YOUR
IDENTITY
ZONES

ALSO BY MARK A. WILLIAMS

*The 10 Lenses: Your Guide to Living & Working
in a Multicultural World*

Other titles in Capital's Business & Personal Development series:

All About Earnings: 100 Ways to Profit in the New Economy
by The Profit Advisors, Barry Schimel, CPA; Gary Kravitz,
and Barry J. Friedman, CPA

The New Talk Power: The Mind-Body Way to Speak like a Pro
by Natalie H. Rogers, M.S.W., C.S.W.

Nonstop Networking: How to Improve Your Life, Luck and Career
by Andrea Nierenberg

*The Protocol School of Washington's The Power of Handshaking:
For Peak Performance Worldwide*
by Robert E. Brown and Dorothea Johnson

*The Protocol School of Washington's Etiquette Intelligence:
The Ultimate International Business Tool*
by Dorothea Johnson and Robert Hickey

Save 25 percent when you order any of these and other fine Capital titles
from our Web site: www.capital-books.com.

YOUR
IDENTITY
ZONES

WHO AM I?

WHO ARE YOU?
HOW DO WE GET ALONG?

MARK A. WILLIAMS

A MarkusWorks Book

CAPITAL
BOOKS, INC.
Sterling, Virginia

Capital Books, Inc.
P.O. Box 605
Herndon, Virginia 20172-0605

ISBN 1-931868-90-5 (alk.paper)

Library of Congress Cataloging-in-Publication Data

Williams, Mark Alexander.
    Your identity zones : Who am I? Who are you? How do we get along? /
Mark A. Williams.—1st ed.
        p.   cm.
    ISBN 1-931868-90-5 (alk. paper)
    1. Identity (Psychology)—Social aspects.   2. Interpersonal relations.
    I. Title.

    BF697.5.S65W55   2004
    158.2—dc22

                                                    2004011968

Printed in the United States of America on acid-free paper that meets the American National Standards Institute Z39-48 Standard.

Book design and composition by Susan Mark
Coghill Composition Company
Richmond, Virginia

First Edition

10   9   8   7   6   5   4   3   2   1

Acknowledgments

This book is dedicated to my family—**Laurie, Lukas,** and **Alexander**— for the unconditional love and deep joy they bring me. Their patience and encouragement is a gift. I would also like to acknowledge the friends and colleagues who made this work possible:

Donna Oetzel:
Without your intuitive, intellectual, and creative collaboration, this book would not have come to life. Your ability to communicate with clarity and passion is magical.

Caroline Spinelli:
Thanks for your unconditional trust, fellowship, and professionalism.

Terry McPherson:
Your unwavering resolve and dedication to the work are inspirational. Thanks again for being a brother.

Evan Harvey:
You brought innovation, intelligence, and focus to this project.

Michael Knopf:
You caught the vision and provided a gentle landing.

Milo Pinckney:
Thanks for awakening the warrior within.

Len Wisneski:
You opened the door to a new future.

Alejandro Alberto Gonzales:
You are my true friend, even through the darkest hours.

Mel Warriner
Thanks for being a creative and conspiratorial partner.

Chandra Irvin:
You are my "sister guide."

Muriel Nellis:
Thanks for your unwavering advocacy.

Jane Roberts:
Thanks for holding my hand.

Kyla Rudman:
Your vision inspires me.

Contents

PART 3: READING RELATIONSHIPS

PART 4: CROSSING THE ZONES

PART 5: KNOWING YOUR PURPOSE

Foreword

Imagine yourself somewhere in southern France in the 1400s. New towns, cities, markets, ships from faraway places, new people—lots of new people. Your world has suddenly, dramatically changed. Thousands are leaving the stultifying, but familiar, life of the farm and field, and moving into these new and exiting places. Peasants are now townspeople. A new class of bourgeoisie has been created seemingly overnight. Old titles of nobility matter less and less. It is all about cash, making it, accumulating it, spending it, and investing it. New ideas to develop. New worlds to conquer. New technologies to be invented. The individual will reign. Eventually, going with the flow, old elites will be just names.

Think about all of the adjustments having to be made. New people mean new relationships—employer–employee, investor–creator, cities–neighbors. New opportunities, new ways of living and seeing things—the accent is on the new, not tradition; on the individual, not family; on cash wealth, not land.

This renaissance from feudalism to capitalism took hundreds of years. In some ways, feudalism still exists in peoples' lives in the West. It definitely exists in many of today's developing countries. Yet, this dynamic transition has taken a long time.

But, just stop and think about your life today. New technologies that were not even around fifteen, ten, even five years ago now dominate. Some of those brand new technologies are in their second and third generation today—and are still changing. Just as the birth of capitalism ushered in a brave new world of exploration, new lands and peoples, and exciting new ideas, today's world of telecommunications, biotechnology, and nanotechnology are creating generations that last only months.

Today we have transcended and rendered obsolete old definitions of space and geography. We are global. Our kids are upstairs communicating with teens in São Paolo, Beijing, and Singapore. This is the world of global communications, smart bombs, global music, CNN, and so on. Classrooms and workplaces all over the world are populated with new immigrants from China, Africa, Latin America, the Middle East.

But still there are the questions that have dogged us homo sapiens from the beginning—Who am I? How do I fit in? What is she thinking? What makes him tick? Why does he act so differently? Should I hire her? Should I fire him? How will she respond if I say this? Why did he act like that when I said that?

Relationships at work, at play, in school, at parties, in traffic still drive us crazy. But how do we best grasp those around us? How do we best understand the guy next door? The woman in cubicle four? The girl standing alone in the corner? The man in the mirror? Especially in a world that is constantly changing all around us.

Thank God for Mark Williams. His newest book, *Your Identity Zones*, is our guide for this new global village and workplace. This book will be as useful to a wide range of professionals and people-watchers as Gail Sheehy's *Passages*, John Nesbitt's *Megatrends*, and any of Alvin Toffler's works. I like this book for three reasons. First, it sets the stage by defining this new era of change and cogently arguing for new ways to see how people function in and react to it. Second, it empowers me as an employer to personally and professionally navigate these new waters. And, finally, it incorporates the most sophisticated polling and cluster analysis to determine what really matters to people.

It is that last point that I especially want to emphasize. As a pollster, I am often asked about why people support or oppose a candidate or an issue, or why they vote the way they do. How will Catholics react? Do Muslims support President Bush? Is it true that about 30 percent of born-again Christians vote Democrat and consider themselves to be liberal? Did union voters really vote for Ronald Reagan? Mark Williams's thesis and research underscores the answers I have always given to these and similar types of questions: it is one thing to be categorized within a group. It is another thing entirely to suggest that belonging to that group is your principal identifier or driver that determines how you will vote or react.

The usefulness of this book is that it offers a roadmap for the CEO, the human resources manager, the party host and hostess, the teacher, the club member. By identifying a new paradigm for understanding human relationships, decisions, emotions, and reactions and sensitivities in this new era of perpetual change, Williams has presented us with a valuable tool that will surely be used in training seminars and teacher orientation programs for years to come.

Your Identity Zones is a vital, practical contribution to understanding human behavior.

John Zogby, President/CEO
Zogby International

Introduction

This book describes a method—a framework—for understanding yourself and connecting with others. This framework can open up new ways of thinking about your identity, improve relationships in all areas of your life, and build your confidence when interacting with different people.

Why do we need this new approach? Changes in contemporary society are forcing us to redefine the concept of identity. Old ways of understanding and interacting—with friends, family, colleagues, and our selves—are proving less successful as society evolves. As the number of acceptable lifestyles, perspectives, values, and cultural attitudes grows, we must grow with it. I believe we're in transition from one age to another—from the age of the *uni-self* to the age of the *multi-self*. Perhaps this sounds dramatic. But read the profiles of the *uni-self* and *multi-self* below, and you may come to share my belief that this societal shift is inevitable.

The Uni-self

The uni-self was a product of the twentieth century. The uni-self lived and worked in homogeneous communities, where there was consensus about the proper roles for men and women. "Families" were rigidly defined and certain religious, racial, and class boundaries were implacable. The uni-self was formed and operated within the confines of national borders, and it tolerated little dissent when it came to conventional notions of right and wrong.

The uni-self categorized and treated people according to easily identifiable affiliations: Black, Asian, male, female, Christian, Jew, American, upper class, middle class, foreigner, et cetera. Affiliations such as gender, race, and religion were as rigid as national borders, and one could not easily break out of conventional definitions to express inner longings and individuality. We related to people as though their values, beliefs, perspectives, and aspirations came entirely from one or two aspects of their identity.

The Multi-self

The multi-self lives in a time of individuality, accelerated by rapid globalization and multiculturalism. Conventional definitions of family, work, age, nationality, sexuality, and gender are constantly evolving. The multi-self lives and works with immigrants, divorcés and divorcées, gays, lesbians, single parents, and the physically disabled. Television, international media outlets, the World Wide Web, twenty-four-hour news channels, and niche market stations bring different values and cultures right into our home. In this curious new era, blue-collar millionaires may never finish high school and highly educated bluebloods go looking for work. Twenty-five-year-olds may be asked to supervise—and reprimand—employees thirty years their senior.

What's more, a strong belief in individual freedom has emerged. The multi-self has little choice but to deal with an expansion of tolerable and acceptable values, openly expressed by empowered individuals. Thus, the multi-self lives in an age of accelerated individuality. The dynamic marketplace has rushed to recognize, legitimize, and serve the needs and sensibilities of new consumers with alternative values and beliefs. The economic viability of those outside the mainstream has driven the multi-society toward acceptance of diverse individuality.

Relationships in the age of the multi-self are in transition, too. The multi-self must move beyond political correctness and develop the environments, norms, and skills to forge authentic relationships with all kinds of people. In the age of the multi-self, flexibility, openness, and people skills have become the essential tools for success. The health and well-being of the multisociety depends on our ability to bridge differences and forge connections. Just as the quest for individuality is accelerating, treating people with tolerance and respect has become a social, professional, and global imperative.

How Can the Identity Zones Help You?

The Identity Zones framework is a tool for the new age. It can help you appreciate the subtle differences in individual perspectives and values. It allows you to learn about real people, in real time, and understand the process as ongoing, dynamic, and rewarding. By the time you finish this book, you will be able to:

- Measure key aspects of your identity in five Identity Zones (temperature, circle of inclusion, commitment, strategy, and power)
- Assess strengths and weaknesses based on your Identity Zones.
- Understand how to "read" family members, friends, clients, and colleagues using Identity Zones.
- Understand how to read organizations, communities, and nations using Identity Zones.
- Learn skills and techniques to connect with others and deal with zone-related interpersonal conflict.
- Examine your life experiences in a deeper, more holistic context using a sixth zone (purpose).

To put this all into perspective, you'll find charts throughout the book that reveal the results of the Zogby International Identity Zones Survey, conducted in March 2004, from interviews with 1,006 adults chosen at random nationwide, ages eighteen to seventy plus. Using the five Identity Zones—temperature, circle of inclusion, strategy, commitment, and power—those surveyed were questioned regarding their feelings on line of work, gender, nationality, race, faith, political affiliation, and parental status. Among many fascinating results, the Zogby survey revealed that offensive comments about a person's faith triggered the most intense responses (56 percent), followed by attacks on parental status (44 percent). Least likely to generate an intense response were attacks on political affiliation (20 percent) or line of work (20 percent). And, except for religion and parental status, a majority of those surveyed indicated that offensive comments about all other factors "left them cold."

As I have, I hope you will see this book as a journey. You decide how to approach it: whether to charge ahead from start to finish, or take it slowly, meandering back and forth, stopping frequently to rest your mind. Either way, you'll have plenty of food for thought. You will encounter interesting individuals, strangers now, but they will soon seem quite familiar. This book is filled with real stories about real people, all searching to understand themselves and connect with others.

We'll begin with a story of my own.

Part 1

GETTING STARTED

I grew up in Virginia Beach, Virginia, in the late 1960s, in a society that was still divided by race. The school system had only recently been integrated. Day by day, week by week, I coped with the legacy of racial discrimination and struggled with what it meant to be Black in the American South. It was a difficult and painful time. My race defined my experience and formed the center of my identity.

When I was twelve, I was diagnosed with a hereditary degenerative disease called Charcot-Marie Tooth, which affects the nervous system and leads to atrophy of the lower extremities. As you can imagine, this news came as quite a shock to an adolescent boy. The emergence of my disability and gradual acceptance of new limitations were facts of life, forced into my emerging identity.

As the disease progressed, I learned to hide my disability. I compensated for my slight limp and rarely showed my legs in public. I was extremely sensitive about my condition and tried to avoid being teased, slighted, or pitied. This approach was reinforced by both the overt attitudes and subtle clues that I picked up from my family and society about being a boy: "Hide your weakness," they said. I got so good at hiding that I didn't think of myself as disabled. It was no longer part of my identity—at least not at a conscious level. The disease went dormant when I was sixteen, enabling me to live the next thirty years in partial denial.

During those years, as I changed and matured, I was always redefining my identity. Over time, I added new important aspects to it, in addition to my race: I became a husband, father, creative artist, author, consultant, and entrepreneur. As I approached middle age, I began to feel that I had "come into my own," and I felt a sense of self-confidence and empowerment in many areas of my life. But my self-image was about to change again. In my mid-forties, the degenerative disease "woke up." My legs began to re-atrophy. My days of masquerading as a physically adroit man were coming to an end.

Life has a way of getting past our mental blocks. It either chips them away, piece by piece, or knocks them down with one big blow. Facing renewed challenges, my covering behaviors faded, and my sense of denial melted away. No longer a teenager, I found I had neither the energy nor the desire to keep disappearing behind convenient pretext. I was tired of inventing excuses for avoiding outdoor activities, tired of explaining away the frustration and exhaustion I experienced during business travel. I had always placed a premium on privacy, self-reliance, and pride. But now I value authenticity and intimacy even more. For the first time, I considered opening myself up to a network of disabled activists and friends. Masking my challenges had allowed me to conceal my disability, but it also prevented me from developing self-awareness and support.

As often happens in life, adversity became a pathway for understanding and development. I haven't found it easy to cope with the return of a painful condition. But I credit this major life change, and the process of reassessment and revision that came with it, as instrumental to the writing of this book. I knew I had undergone a profound shift in my identity. When I first shared the story of my disability, many lifelong friends and colleagues were shocked. To them, it seemed as if they had to get to know me all over again. They had to reassess every aspect of our interactions, to reincorporate "the new me," which needed new sensitivities. And I had to do the same. We all experience "identity shifts" throughout our lives, but usually it happens gradually, without a dramatic moment of revelation.

1

The Origins of
Identity Zones

Identity Zones picks up a line of thinking that I initiated in my first book, *The 10 Lenses: Your Guide to Living and Working in a Multicultural World*. In *The 10 Lenses* I focused exclusively on race, ethnicity, and cultural differences. I tried to go beyond the limitations of racial demographics, the categories that too often lead us to talk sweepingly about "what Blacks think," or "what Hispanics think," and so on. Instead, I looked for commonalities in feelings, beliefs, values, perspectives, and behaviors. I identified ten distinctly different views—or "lenses"—such as the *Meritocratist* view or the *Assimilationist* view, which cut across racial and ethnic lines.

Like the *10 Lenses*, the Identity Zones framework incorporates cultural differences, but it goes much further. The framework provides a way to understand yourself and others by zoning in on innate characteristics, cultural differences, life circumstances, personal histories, beliefs and values, and deeper philosophies about life purpose. This multidimensional view helps us interpret the world in a comprehensive way, and is tailor made for the multi-self.

As you're reading this introduction, "meeting" me for the first time, how valuable is it to know that I'm an African American man? Isn't it more valuable to know *how I feel* about being an African American man, and how that affects my life? To really connect with me, you might want to know how I feel about other aspects of my identity, too, such as being an adopted child, a father of two young sons, or a person with a physical disability. You might also wonder how my values (such as self-reliance, creativity, and authenticity) influence my behavior. To build a successful relationship with me, you must respect my personal complexity and the richness of my life experiences. To connect more deeply, you must appreciate the multiple aspects of my identity, the true things that reveal my heart and soul.

I believe that trying to comprehend the multidimensional nature of identity is preferable to living in a world where, more often than not, we cope with differences through politically correct manners. In my work with communities and large corporations, I find that many people seem paralyzed by the "politically correct" stance. They walk on eggshells in order to avoid causing any distress or harm. They ritualistically relate to others by using the right words, avoiding risky humor, and relying on notions we think to be true about "them." When I scratch beneath the surface of the polite manners and correct language, however, I find people who are confused, uncomfortable, and reluctant to interact with confidence across differences.

If we focus on feelings, thoughts, perspectives and behaviors—not just demographics—we can begin to dismantle *uni-relationships* and political correctness. Obviously, I'm not suggesting we replace the PC approach by giving everyone a license to be rude and uncaring. But when we learn to understand individuals and their unique sensitivities, we can put aside simplistic notions and treat visible differences as the beginning of a dialogue—not the sum total of our interaction.

I think we've made tremendous progress in the past ten or fifteen years, translating the gains of the Civil Rights era into an ever-increasing awareness of identity. Given our historical record in dealing with differences, this is astonishing progress. But we still have a long way to go.

Conflicts and misunderstandings plague us at home, at work, in our communities, and around the world. We've evolved to the point where we are ready for new skills, new tools, and new strategies that address conflict at a deeper level and put more authentic connections within our grasp. Consider this book the first step on that journey.

2

Using the Framework: A Brief Orientation

I'd like to familiarize you with some of the key terms and concepts I will use as we progress through the book. Fresh language helps me organize my thoughts and express new ideas. I hope it will do the same for you. Among my family, friends, clients, and colleagues, the following terms are now constantly at play and have led to rich and rewarding discussions.

Affiliations are aspects of our identities such as race, gender, marital status, religion, political affiliation, and education. Affiliations describe facts about your life—your innate characteristics, your life choices, your life circumstances, your membership in a category or group. We're often born into affiliations. Some, such as religion or marital status, we can change. Others, such as race or ethnicity, we can't. Because so many are historically charged and/or legally protected, and are the subject of open conflict in our society, I consider affiliations to be the cornerstone of the Identity Zones framework. In this book, we'll be working with twenty-one

9

different Affiliations. You'll be asked to take a brief test to determine how you rank and/or prioritize your personal affiliations.

Values are aspects of our identities, too. In this book, I use the term values to describe deeply held principles such as honesty, security, patriotism, service, and family. They typically grow out of our life experiences and circumstances. But values aren't necessarily tied to the concrete facts about our lives. We get into trouble when we assume certain values are "married" to certain affiliations. Values are mutable and invisible to the casual observer, which often makes them an element of surprise in our interactions with others. There are lots and lots of different ways to talk about values. I've created a list for you to work from, but you are free to add or edit as you see fit.

Identity Zones are five distinct ways to measure the role your affiliations and values play in your life. The five identity zones include:

- **The Temperature Zone**, which measures the strength of your feelings about an affiliation or value, on a continuum from hot to cold.
- **The Inclusion Zone**, which measures the degree to which you use an affiliation or value as a criteria for forming relationships, on a continuum from closed to open.
- **The Commitment Zone**, which measures your commitment to action and change on issues related to an affiliation or value, on a continuum from active to passive.
- **The Strategy Zone,** which measures the type of action you're likely to take to produce change on issues related to an affiliation or value, on a continuum from transformational to conformist.
- **The Power Zone,** which measures your perceived level of power when defending your position or advocating for change on issues related to an affiliation or value, on a continuum from high to low.

There's also a sixth identity zone, which we'll discuss in the last chapter of the book. **The Purpose Zone** measures your philosophical and spiritual approach to an affiliation or value, on a continuum from self to soul.

Most people find it helpful to envision these zones as physical places. Maybe you'll think of your affiliations and values as houses, and identity zones as rooms within each house. I use the term *continuum* here because I don't mean to describe a precise system of measurement, but a sliding scale, a wide-open zone that you can move across as you move across a room, from one door to another. In this book you'll be asked to choose a house (an affiliation or value such as gender or honesty) and decide where you stand, roughly, in each of its rooms (zones). To help you do this, we use a chart like the one below.

Temperature	Hot	Warm	Cold
Circle of Inclusion	Closed	Selective	Open
Commitment	Activist	Engaged	Passive
Strategy	Transform	Reform	Conform
Power	High	Medium	Low

In conversation, we typically shorthand the chart this way: *I'm hot on gender, she's closed on race, he's engaged on community service, you're an activist on political affiliation, my perceived power on religion is high.* But you should keep in mind that it's okay to be in between the boxes on the chart. I sometimes use terms like *warm-hot* or *warm-cold*, for example, to describe middle places within the temperature continuum. And I use *red-hot* or *ice cold* to describe the outer extremes.

Heat Waves and **Cold Fronts.** Sometimes people *cluster* at the left or right side of the identity zones chart. A *heat wave* is someone who tends toward the left side of the chart, meaning he is not only hot, but closed, activist, transformational . . . someone who is extremely passionate and committed about a particular affiliation or value. *Cold fronts* tend toward the cold side of the chart and have no strong feelings or no interest in engaging about a particular affiliation or value. If you've got a *heat wave personality*, you're extremely sensitive about several affiliations or values; a *cold front personality* is disengaged on many affiliations and values.

Zone Hotspots (Zots). What are *zots*? They're parts of your identity that you're extremely sensitive about. When someone touches your zots, you get angry, hurt, frustrated, annoyed, afraid, and defensive. I use the term *zots* because it reminds us that sensitivities and conflict can arise from anywhere within the zone chart, from temperature on down through power.

Triggers, Red Flags, and **Blowouts.** In this book we'll talk a great deal about zone-based conflict. *Triggers* are jokes, offhand comments, workplace policies, and political speeches—anything that inflames somebody's zot and becomes a potential source of conflict. *Red flags* are signs that a zone-based conflict is brewing. *Blowouts* are major zone-based conflicts—typically face-to-face arguments—with potentially damaging consequences.

The Multi-self. This framework is based on the notion that we are evolving toward the age of the *multi-self* (see page xvi). I will use this term throughout the book. But I think it's important to note that the *multi* trends I've identified aren't happening everywhere. Some countries are still primarily *uni* in their societal as well as individual views of identity. Many of the statements I make in this book may strike you as most relevant to "first world" countries—those that have been most impacted by the collision of social and economic forces known as globalization. But the basic premise of Identity Zones—being sensitive to people's values and cultural perspectives—can apply to anyone anywhere.

This should be enough to help you navigate the chapters ahead. One last thing you should know: I've been fortunate to work in partnership with Zogby International, a leader in the field of polling and public opinion, on studying the Identity Zones framework and creating research-based indicator tests. If you'd like to take the Identity Zones indicators and learn more about applications for this framework in schools, businesses, and communities, please visit www.identityzones.com.

Part 2

KNOWING YOURSELF

He who knows others is wise;
He who knows himself is enlightened.

—Lao-tzu, *The Way of Lao-tzu*

We can better understand and connect with others if we understand ourselves. Easier said than done! Self-exploration should be a lifelong process. But too often we operate on autopilot, using outdated patterns and worn-out habits, long after the conditions and requirements for success have fundamentally changed. When we use old maps to travel across new territories, we tend to get lost in the complexities of the multiworld.

If you know more about who you are, you can understand why certain types of beliefs and behaviors—even the subtlest of slights—can provoke strong emotions and feelings of anger, fear, or hurt. Rather than being caught off guard and offering a knee-jerk reaction, you will be able to do some advance reconnaissance. You can anticipate potential problems because you know your zots, and can more strategically and gracefully choose the best response in a moment of conflict.

Before any journey begins, you must know where you are—your point of origin. And it can also be useful to know what brought you to that point. These are the two main goals for this section: to know where you are today and understand how you got here.

By the time we're done, you will know:

- How you prioritize the key affiliations and values in your life today
- How to measure the role these affiliations and values play in your life through five identity zones (temperature, circle of inclusion, commitment, strategy, and power)
- What you need to know about your place on each zone continuum
- How your past influences your affiliations, values, and zones

15

As you move through the book I provide you with some suggested exercises, which I think will help you grasp the concepts and put the framework into practice. By the end of part 2 you'll have the tools to create a full identity zone chart for any of your affiliations and values, or a portrait of one or more aspects of your identity.

3

Affiliations
and Values

Who am I? Who are you? How can we begin to answer such questions? Each human being is a distinct blend of DNA, created at the moment of conception, long before we had any say in the matter. But in this multiworld, we define ourselves by our life choices as well as our genetic destinies, blending the two to create a sense of self. We express ourselves through where we work, who we love, how we look, what we believe, where we came from, when we were born. We define ourselves according to a combination of affiliations and values, some obvious to others at first glance, others not. Think about race and gender, for example, versus sexual orientation, parental status, educational background, or nationality. Think, too, about the values that guide us through life, like fidelity or humility or professionalism. Our identity may be shaped by what's apparent to the naked eye. But our multidimensionality guarantees that we can't be understood at first glance.

When we meet people, most of us consciously or unconsciously go digging for shared affiliations and values. As the father of two children, for example, I often find it easy to strike up a conversation with other parents.

Sometimes our shared affiliation—parental status—becomes the starting point for a relationship. As any parent knows, sometimes you need to confide the fears and frustrations of parenting with others "in the same boat," bonding through laughter, comfort, childcare advice, and companionship. In some cases, the spark ignited by a commonality leads to a deeper relationship, uniting two families in an enduring bond.

Here's another example of the role shared affiliations and values play in my own life: I value the arts and tend to surround myself with people who share this value, whether they're writers, musicians, artists, performers, educators, aspiring actors, or simply "creative spirits." I like to find others who share my enthusiasm for creative pursuits. I'm always on the lookout for collaborators and inspirational figures.

Okay, so I'm a parent who values creativity. Does that mean that I automatically get along with all creative-minded parents? Obviously not. Commonalities can be powerful connectors, but remember what we said at the beginning: human beings are multidimensional. A single affiliation cannot define me—even two affiliations won't do it. Beyond parenthood, beyond creativity, I have many other affiliations and values.

What's more, I prioritize my affiliations and values in my own unique way. This is one of the key ideas behind the framework: not all affiliations are created equal. When we're thinking about the affiliations and values in our lives, prioritizing sheds light on where we stand *today*. It's a good way to be honest with ourselves about who we are now, without getting hung up on an outdated self-image. Does parental status define me more than my other key affiliations, such as my gender? What about my religious beliefs? Are the arts more important to me than loyalty, education, or family? Simply knowing which aspects of identity are most important to us can give us fresh insight—a powerful tool when we seek to understand other people and avoid conflict.

A Note about Values

It's important to note that this framework is designed to take both affiliations and values into account. Affiliations often play a starring role today in the zone-based conflicts that make the most headlines—the multimillion-dollar lawsuits, the debates about politics and language, the global strife that affects us all. But I created this framework because I believe we can't separate affiliations from values, at least not if we want an accurate understanding of real people and situations. If you'll recall from my story about my experiences with Charcot-Marie Tooth disease, you'll note that for much of my life, I placed a high priority on the values of privacy and self-reliance, which made me downplay my affiliation on disability. As I got older, my identity shifted and my priorities changed. I placed a higher priority on the value of authenticity and I began to embrace my affiliation on physical disability. Values and affiliations were inexorably linked in this progression.

In my work with large organizations, I've seen conflicts completely misread because they seemed to be clashes between affiliations, when they really had more to do with values. A manager I know, a Hispanic man, was very upset when one of the vice presidents of his company tried to paint a rosy picture of the company's future by exaggerating the truth in a press release. The partner responsible for the release was white, and some people interpreted the conflict between the two men as a racial one. But for the manager, the conflict was over honesty and integrity, two of his core values. He had taken consistent stands within the organization on issues like this before, and he was surprised when the situation was viewed through a racial lens.

A conflict over an affiliation like race is an attention-grabber in today's businesses. But we don't help matters when we take the easy way out, reacting to complex situations based on this single affiliation.

Exercise 1: Prioritizing Your Affiliations

You will see a list of affiliations below. Much debate went into the creation of this list, but it is by no means comprehensive or complete. The list highlights affiliations that are important to people across many cultures and lifestyles, and I believe that it serves the purposes of this book.

To begin, review the affiliations list by reading through it quickly. Then go back and assign a letter grade to indicate the importance of each affiliation to your sense of identity: "A" indicates high importance, "B" indicates moderate importance, and "C" indicates low importance or irrelevance.

This exercise will prepare you for the rest of the exercises in this section of the book. Be sure to choose an affiliation that you believe is central to your life, something rooted in the core of your being. (Note: You can repeat this process with one of your "B" or "C" affiliations and contrast the results.)

Affiliations A = High; B = Moderate; C = Low	Importance
Race. Your racial heritage, if you identify yourself as part of a racial group (e.g., black or African American, white or Caucasian, American Indian, Biracial, Multiracial)	
Ethnicity. Your ethnic background, if you identify yourself as part of an ethnic group based on a combination of traits such as religion, race, national origin, or culture (e.g., Latino, Asian, Serbian, Kurdish)	
Nationality. The nation where you live as a legal citizen, whether by birth or naturalization	
Gender. Your sex (male, female, or transgender)	
Age. Your chronological age or membership in a particular age group (e.g., child, teenager, middle-aged, elder)	
Physical Ability. Your ability to perform physical tasks, frequently described in terms of challenges or limitations (blindness, using a wheelchair, etc.)	
Sexual Orientation. Your preference in sexual partners (e.g., gay, lesbian, heterosexual, bisexual)	
Religion. Your beliefs concerning the cause, nature, and purpose of the universe; your affiliation with a church, synagogue or other religious institution; your religious background (e.g., Catholic, Jewish, Muslim, Buddhist, Agnostic, Atheist)	

Affiliations	Importance
Education. Your academic record and/or degrees earned; the prestige of the school(s) you attended; your level of education as demonstrated by the breadth of your knowledge or skill in certain subjects	
Socioeconomic Status. Your current financial situation; your degree of financial success; your place on the socioeconomic ladder, as defined by a combination of social and economic factors that may include your ethnicity, your education, your class, and your profession	
Physical Appearance. Your looks as measured by societal norms; the degree to which you're considered attractive or physically fit; your physical traits (e.g., weight, height, hair color)	
Marital Status. Married, unmarried, divorced, single, widowed	
Parental Status. New mother, father of three, single parent, parent of an adopted child, no children by choice, no children due to health or circumstance	
Regional Affiliation. Where you currently live or where you were born; your community, your state, your district, your geographical area (Brooklyn, Texas, the Bay Area)	
Profession. Your occupation, career, or affiliation with a group of skilled professionals (e.g., welder, child care provider, musician, attorney, professor)	
Political Affiliation. Your political beliefs, especially if you adhere to the social, economic, and political platform of a specific party (Democratic, Republican) or ideological stance (conservative, liberal)	
Organizational Level. Your role in the hierarchy of a company or organization (e.g., administrative, midlevel manager, executive)	
Military Experience. Your military training and experience, if any	

(continued)

Affiliations	Importance
Class. Your social position as defined by economic, political, or cultural characteristics (lower, middle, upper middle, upper)	
Family of Origin. Your parents, family history, or genealogical roots reaching back a number of generations	
Recognition/Acclaim. Your reputation; the degree to which you are recognized or celebrated within a larger group (your profession, your workplace, your community, society at large)	

Exercise 2: Prioritize Your Values

Now that you've completed the affiliations exercise above, let's repeat the process with a list of values. Remember: mark "A" if the value is highly important to you, "B" if it is moderately important, and "C" if the value is not important or irrelevant.

Values	Importance
Honesty Telling the truth in all situations Being clear, precise, and truthful with everyone An absolute fidelity for the truth in any form	
Humor Enjoying laughter, good times, and lightheartedness Speaking, acting, and interacting in a fun or funny manner A reluctance to take life too seriously	
Generosity Giving oneself or one's resources to others The free donation of goods/services to a worthy cause, group, person	
Self-Reliance Making it based on your own efforts without dependence on others	

Values	Importance
Depending on oneself for sustenance, advancement, and success A refusal to accept unnecessary outside assistance	
Security Making choices to ensure physical, emotional, and financial safety Valuing the known over the unknown, safety over risk	
Fidelity Commitment to one sexual partner Strong adherence to a single person, object, or idea	
Love of Country Honoring and sacrificing to keep your country strong Dominant loyalty to—and belief in—one's home nation Political, social, and economic allegiance to a single country	
Social Justice/Equality Ensuring that everyone is treated with dignity and respect and fairness Commitment to equal opportunities for all people A willingness to advocate for equity in social and legal systems	
Leisure/Fun Preference for a relaxed, recreation-oriented lifestyle Belief in a strong separation between work time and personal time Defines oneself by leisure activities, not work accomplishments	
Morality Strict definition and observance of right vs. wrong Disapproves of behavior that breaks traditional societal norms Believes that our actions are judged by a higher power	
Sports/Adventure Direct or indirect participation in teams, activities, and exercise Defining oneself by actions, not thoughts or words	

(continued)

Values	Importance
Arts/Creativity Enjoyment of theater, dance, music, movies and other creative arts Individual and collective support of creative arts and artists The expression of one's spirit and one's interpretation of the world	
Power Desire to control the fate of individuals or circumstances Respect for dominance, leadership, and authority Allegiance to strength, wealth, or political dominance	
Prestige Cherishing the recognition of one's own accomplishments Placing a high premium on historical or traditional excellence Valuing public adulation and/or approval	
Friendship Maintaining connection, commitment, and intimacy with certain people Stronger loyalty to individuals over groups Uses personal relationships as the basis for most dealings	
Service Helping others with a sense of mission and compassion Donation of one's time and energy to a greater cause Belief in the power of principled, directed, hard work	
Competition Engaging in activities to excel and win Defining oneself in relation to the strengths and weaknesses of others Belief in the survival of the fittest	
Money Accumulating financial resources Gaining material wealth is a high—and noble—aspiration	
Education Earning degrees in order to master a subject area Life is a process of continual learning Knowledge gained means more than wealth, power	

Values	Importance
Physical Fitness/Appearance Staying in good physical condition Making lifestyle choices that preserve/project a positive physical image Good clothes, a sense of style, dressing appropriately	
Belonging/Fitting In Enjoys associating with—and being liked by—others Reluctance to stand out or be noticed individually Feeling at home in comfortable, traditional groups	
Nature Cultivating a special relationship with the outdoors Believing in the celebration and preservation of the natural world Humans exist in nature, not apart from it	
Integrity Following a personal, moral, or ethical standard An internal "honor code" that guides all life choices Our beliefs about right and wrong should dictate our behaviors	
Reputation Protecting the good name that you have earned through past deeds Enjoying notoriety through a legacy of excellence	
World Peace Striving to solve cultural, national, religious or other global conflicts A strong belief in the interconnectedness of all nations and peoples	
Fairness Ensuring that the rules are applied consistently in all situations Acknowledging that equity is the ideal outcome	
Structure Routines, processes, and policies are predictable and consistent Commitments are kept	

(continued)

Values	Importance
Creating a plan and sticking to it will produce the best result	
Responsibility Bearing the burden for economic, political, social, and other outcomes Wielding both the power and the judgment to ensure success Not blaming others for organizational failures	
Intimacy Deep, meaningful, and soulful connection with another Dropping one's guard emotionally, intellectually, physically	
Independence/Autonomy The ability to control one's own actions No need to heed the wishes, plans, words, or actions of others	
Courtesy The display of good manners and politeness Acknowledging others even when it is unnecessary Taking extra time and care to ensure that everyone's needs are met	
Assertiveness The ability to freely state one's needs, desires, and opinions Exerting influence upon situations to serve one's desires	
Individualism/Uniqueness Highlighting or cultivating those personal aspects or attributes that make one stand out or differ from the norm Celebrating the infinite complexity, capacity, and creativity of the individual	
Success Accomplishing goals, earning the payoff, and basking in recognition Goal-oriented behaviors that promote material or personal gains	
Family The joy of membership in a close relational unit A primary allegiance to family relations above all others	

4

The Temperature Zone

Now that you've prioritized your affiliations and values, we're going to move on to talk about Identity Zones. As a reminder, identity zones are distinct ways of measuring the role that an affiliation or value plays in your life. We'll discuss the sixth zone, purpose, which is a bit different from the other zones, at the book's conclusion.

Of the first five zones, temperature is the leader, and the most powerful. This is the zone that tells you how sensitive you are about affiliation or values. What really makes your blood boil? Offensive comments about your gender or profession or age? People who lie? People who "play the victim?" People who flaunt their wealth or status or family background? Temperature is all about how you feel. When you're looking at a high-priority affiliation or value, temperature is a measure of whether you're:

- Hot (very sensitive)
- Warm (somewhat sensitive)
- Cold (not sensitive at all)

Why is this the most powerful zone? Because at the hot end of the temperature continuum, people are more likely to have zone hotspots, or zots, that are triggered during the course of an interaction. Temperature does more than tell us an affiliation or value is a high priority—it also tells us whether there are underlying issues, past or present, that make the affiliation or value a sensitive one.

I consider parental status an "A" affiliation. Let's pretend for a moment that you feel the same way. We have something in common. But this connection, while useful, only scratches the surface of our identity as parents. We don't necessarily "wear" our affiliations in the same way. There are a variety of ways to be a parent, a variety of life circumstances that can change our feelings about parenting, and a variety of zots that are unique to each individual parent. If all I know is that you're a parent, and that parenting is important to you, here are some things I don't know:

- Are you a single parent?
- Are you raising an adopted child?
- Is your child a scholarship student at an elite private school?
- Are you the parent of a biracial child?
- Does your child live far away, with your divorced spouse, in another state or country?
- Are you an orthodox Jew, Muslim, or Catholic, raising your children in a community that doesn't seem to understand or respect your faith?
- Do you have other high-priority affiliations or values that make this one (parental status) more challenging or difficult for you?

To illustrate this point, let me tell you a bit about Dana, who gave birth to her first child last year. Her parental status, once of little consequence, has become a much higher priority in her life. Parenting has raised lots of new, challenging issues for her at home, in the workplace, and in the community. She is a committed parent who sometimes feels lost at sea, struggling to define herself in the face of personal and societal pressures and expectations. Here's what Dana has to say, in her own words, about becoming a parent:

On the day my son was born, I feel like I developed a third eye, a third ear, and a second nose. My "mommy senses" are impossible to turn off. Suddenly I can hear crying babies everywhere—not only my own, but the one who lives three houses over. I'm a hawk when it comes to news, information, and attitudes about parenting. All my life I've seen myself as a woman who puts her career and her independence first. Now I'm determined to strive for excellence in parenting in addition to my career . . . and I resent any implication that it can't be done.

Dana is sensitive, warm or perhaps hot, on parental status. Someone who didn't know Dana well could say the wrong thing about parenting and find herself on the receiving end of a powerful expression of emotion. Even a parent like me, who places a high priority on my parental status, could inflame tensions by not showing awareness, empathy, or respect for the challenges of her situation. Jokes, dismissive comments, misjudgments of the depth of her feelings—these actions are triggers when you're dealing with the hot end of the temperature continuum. In Dana's case, her response to triggers would be strongly affected by other affiliations and values in her life that are stacked on top of parental status, such as her gender, her professional affiliation, and her convictions about the value of education.

Temperature Indicators

What's your temperature on parental status? On gender? On self-reliance? Most of us can instinctively take our own temperatures, at least for our "A" affiliations and values. Indicators can help you refine your instinctive response. They can also help you when you're trying to assess your temperature on affiliations or values that play a less central role in your life. Remember, we measure identity zones on a continuum. Look at the diagram below. You might fall into the left side of the continuum—somewhere between warm and hot—on race or sexual preference, or into the right side of the zone—somewhere between warm and cold—on honesty or integrity. Your temperature will be different, expressed in different degrees, for each affiliation and value.

Temperature	Hot	Warm	Cold

The indicators for temperature measure your sensitivity based on your feelings and responses to the world around you. They include:

- Media Awareness
- Political/Community Awareness
- Language Awareness
- Humor Sensitivity
- Bonding/Solidarity
- Deeply Held Convictions

Using the example of Dana, we can see how an individual's temperature on parenting might reveal itself through indicators:

Media Awareness. Dana follows the "hot issues" related to parenting (such as prayer in school, day care versus home care, dual-career families) and cares about how they're portrayed in the news, on television, and in popular books and movies.

Political/Community Awareness. Dana is angry about the poor public schools in her neighborhood. She recently attended her first advisory council meeting to learn which local politicians and activists are making a difference.

Language Awareness. She's bothered by terms such as "the mommy track" and "stay-at-home" mom.

Humor Sensitivity. She doesn't appreciate jokes about her parental status, especially in a professional setting, unless they're "inside jokes" by fellow parents.

Bonding/Solidarity. She feels a kinship with fellow parents and looks out for them, helping them navigate challenges and warning them about potential societal or professional inequities.

Deeply Held Convictions. She believes that good parenting is a challenging job that provides important benefits to society as a whole.

These indicators help us see the strong feelings Dana has about parenting, and where some of her sensitivities lie. When we asked Dana to complete the exercise on temperature for her parental status, she charted herself like this:

ZONE: TEMPERATURE
AFFILIATION: PARENTAL STATUS

Temperature	Hot	Warm	Cold

Using indicators doesn't come naturally when you're extremely hot on an affiliation or value. Sometimes, we're so sensitive, any "rational" approach to our feelings feels offensive! But once you get into the habit of using indicators, I think you will find them beneficial. They can help you think about affiliations and values in a more analytical way, stepping back to put your feelings into perspective.

Let me provide another example of how indicators work, this time measuring a value. Jerry, a former member of the military, has a deeply ingrained set of values that guide him in his professional and personal life. One of Jerry's high-priority values is service. He has a sense of mission when it comes to helping others in his community, especially those less fortunate. Here's what Jerry has to say about service as a key value:

> I see kids everyday, out in the streets, with no adult guidance or supervision. I don't care what race they are and neither should anyone else. If they are left alone and drift too long, they will fall prey to negative influences in the environment, like drugs, alcohol, and violence. When that happens, they become an even greater burden for society and we all eventually pay—one way or the other. If everyone did their part to care for these kids who are left unattended, it could make all the difference in the world for them and our communities.

Let's examine Jerry's sensitivities on certain indicators.

Media Awareness. Jerry reads the local newspapers to keep up with news, events, and civic-minded individuals who are making a difference. He is very conscious about his community's unique needs and is sensitive to the ways in which metropolitan media outlets ignore his semirural, semisuburban community—and how they may perpetuate negative stereotypes.

Political/Community Awareness. Jerry supports politicians who seem to have his community's best interests at heart. He admires leaders who demonstrate a commitment to serving the needs of the underprivileged.

Language Awareness. Jerry will bristle at terms like "do-gooder" or "bleeding heart," because they denigrate his hard work and service to others.

Humor Sensitivity. Jerry may joke with insiders about the frustrations of his volunteer work or occasional feelings of futility. But he takes his commitments seriously and doesn't like jokes that minimize his community or his role in making it thrive.

Bonding/Solidarity. Jerry feels a kinship with other service-minded individuals.

Deeply Held Convictions. Jerry is grateful for his successes in life. He believes that we all have a responsibility to reach out to people in need and help them get ahead.

Here is how Jerry placed himself on the temperature continuum for service:

ZONE: TEMPERATURE
VALUE: SERVICE

Temperature	Hot	Warm	Cold

Exercise: Taking Your Temperature

I want you to go back now to your list of high-priority affiliations and values. If you already selected an "A" affiliation or value in the prioritizing exercise, please use that selection. If not, make a selection now. We'll use this affiliation or value for all the exercises through the remainder of part 2. Of course, later, you can go back as often as you choose, repeating the exercises for more affiliations and values.

To take your own temperature, measure your sensitivity on your chosen "A" affiliation or "A" value using these temperature indicators. I've provided some questions to help you with the process. Your answers will determine your place on the temperature continuum. The more emphatically you answer yes (to the yes or no questions), the hotter you are. If you answer yes to certain indicators but not others, you probably fall somewhere in the middle of the continuum. And if you answer no on down the line, place yourself at the cold end of the continuum.

Media Awareness. Am I concerned about how my affiliation/value is portrayed on television, in magazines, and newspapers? Do I read publications directed mostly toward my affiliation/value? Which ones and why?

Political/Community Awareness. Do I support local and national candidates who share my affiliation/value? Do I belong to any community groups focused on empowering/supporting people of my affiliation/value?

Language Awareness. Does it bother me when others use outdated or disparaging terms to describe my affiliation/value?

Humor Sensitivity. Am I sensitive when people make jokes about my affiliation/value?

Bonding/Solidarity. Do I feel a strong connection to people who share my affiliation/value? Do I empathize with their challenges and relate to them as my own?

Deeply Held Convictions. Do I have strong ideas and opinions about my affiliation/value?

After you've spent some time thinking about these questions, you may find additional indicators that help you gauge your temperature. Terrific! The idea is to give yourself enough data to make an accurate assessment of your sensitivity to the affiliation or value you selected. Now you are ready to chart your temperature. It's easiest to use a pencil or crayon for this exercise. Shade or color the appropriate chart below to indicate where you think you fall within the temperature continuum.

ZONE: TEMPERATURE
AFFILIATION: _____

Temperature	Hot	Warm	Cold

ZONE: TEMPERATURE
VALUE: _____

Temperature	Hot	Warm	Cold

Temperature Implications

Why is it important to know your temperature? Let's look closely at the section you colored in the temperature zone. This represents your degree of sensitivity, or your relative lack of sensitivity, about an aspect of your identity.

All areas of the zone have *implications* when you're interacting with others. We'll go into much more detail about methods for handling interactions later. For now, though, it's a good idea to familiarize yourself with the chart below, which lists some of the implications of the hot, warm, and cold areas. The implications are categorized according to strengths and weaknesses. If you're "hot" in the Temperature Zone, for example, your strengths include standing up for your beliefs, refusing to tolerate injustice, and not hesitating to raise important issues. If you're "cold," you may keep your perspective clear and focus on practical solutions.

If your attitude and actions embody the strengths, you will increase the possibility of successful interactions with others. I call this *operating out of your zone strengths*. Operating out of your zone weaknesses, of course, will decrease the possibility of successful interactions. You may not be capable of using your zone strengths in every situation, but if you are aware of your tendencies, you may be able to adjust them in the moment and facilitate a more positive interaction with others.

Zone 1: Temperature Hot Strengths	Zone 1: Temperature Hot Weaknesses
• Voicing the need for increased sensitivity • Standing up for your beliefs • Demanding respect from others • Refusing to tolerate injustice • Challenging authority/status quo • Giving constructive feedback to others • Supporting or speaking up for others	• Ranting and raving • Overly confrontational • Closed and defensive • Resorting to aggression/violence • Undermining/slandering/defaming others • Punishing others through emotional, physical, or spiritual withdrawal • Knee-jerk reactions

Zone 1: Temperature Warm Strengths	Zone 1: Temperature Warm Weaknesses
• Selectively and strategically engaging in issues • Serving as a bridge between others • Able to see and understand both sides • Can see and facilitate finding common ground	• Hiding from the conflict • Not having your voice heard • "Wishy-washy"

Zone 1: Temperature Cold Strengths	Zone 1: Temperature Cold Weaknesses
• Objectivity • Focusing on practical solutions • Diffusing tension between others • Giving helpful advice on social/political boundaries • Open to new information	• Unaware of issues • Fear of engaging • Condescending • Defensive • Not expressing empathy • Moving too quickly to problem-solving mode • Dismissing or overlooking problems • Not investing time or resources • Avoiding/suppressing discussion

Temperature measures how strongly we feel if offensive comments are made—or offensive actions taken—based on our affiliations. In this excerpt from our national survey, notice how people of different nationalities measured faith across the Temperature Zone.

ZONE: TEMPERATURE
AFFILIATION: FAITH

	Central/South American	Southern European	North American Hispanic	Central/Southern African
Hot	70.6%	52.4%	74.0%	72.3%
Warm	0%	20.3%	0%	14.0%
Cold	29.4%	27.3%	26.0%	13.7%

Source: Zogby Survey
03/15/04–03/22/04
Margin of error: +/–3.1%

5

The Circle of Inclusion Zone

Now that you've taken your temperature, we'll move forward to examining your *Circle of Inclusion Zone*, which measures the degree to which you use your affiliations or values to define your social and cultural circle. Who are your friends? Where do you live, shop and socialize? Which colleagues do you ask to lunch? Your high-priority values and affiliations most likely influence these decisions. Circle of Inclusion is about your choices and preferences, not about circumstances you can't control. Looking at an "A" affiliation or value, are you:

- Closed (willing to include only those who share the affiliation/value)
- Selective (willing to include some who don't share the affiliation/value)
- Open (freely including all, regardless of whether they share the affiliation/value)

Generally, I think we have a hard time being honest with ourselves about the Circle of Inclusion Zone. There are several reasons for this. For one thing, openness is becoming a shared societal value in this multiage—at least on the surface. If you take your clues from the TV advertisements and political speeches, the message is clear: we're all expected to embrace difference, to surround ourselves by a "mixed salad" of family, friends, business associates, and neighbors.

Second, whenever we come into contact with public organizations (corporations, schools, government entities), we're reminded that openness is required by law in many instances, made official through diversity initiatives and policies that dictate "inclusive" environments. Finally, I think we tend to think that if we're not willing to be absolutely open, we must be in denial about our deepest feelings, harboring prejudice or snobbery or worse, especially when we're talking about affiliations such as race, gender, class, and religion.

While we all love the idea of being open and accepting, the truth is that we all make selective choices about who we let into our lives, especially into our inner circles. Your personal history and life experiences affect your comfort level with affiliations or values different from your own.

Let me tell you about my lifelong friend Barry. I met Barry in college during the 1970s in Washington, DC. We established a connection immediately, partly because we were both African Americans who saw race as central to our lives, and who tended toward the hot end of the temperature continuum on race. But we differed in the Circle of Inclusion Zone. Barry grew up in the Bronx, in a world that was almost entirely black. Barry preferred to be in social and communal relationships exclusively with other African Americans. He was closed on race. When he was assigned a roommate who happened to be Japanese American, he changed his living arrangements.

Barry had nothing against his roommate—he just wanted to be fully at ease or "let his hair down" in his own room. Barry and I could not always socialize together, because Barry didn't feel he fit in with my multicultural friends. Unlike Barry, I was selective on race, tending toward open. I grew up in predominantly white Virginia Beach. I was in the first class of the first blacks to integrate the local school system. From a young age, I believed integration was desirable, not just in public life, but in private life as well.

Barry and I are still friends today. Over time, I've become more and more open on race. I've sought friends of all ethnicities and cultural backgrounds. Barry has stayed relatively closed. I don't always like Barry's point of view—nor he mine—but I respect his choices and understand his perspective.

Circle of Inclusion Indicators

The indicators for the Circle of Inclusion Zone are:

- Neighborhood/Community
- Critical Service Providers
- Membership in Social Organizations
- Social Life
- Sources of News/Information/Entertainment

Let's use these indicators to take a closer look at my friend Barry based on his current Circle of Inclusion preferences on race.

Neighborhood/Community. Barry lives in a predominately African American community. For socializing, he prefers not to venture too far away from his neighborhood, into other neighborhoods that are racially mixed or "too white."

Critical Service Providers. Barry is a middle-class professional who shops, dines at, and patronizes businesses all over the Washington, DC metropolitan area. But if his needs can be met in his community, he prefers to stay in the neighborhood, where businesses are largely black owned and operated.

Membership in Social Organizations. Barry belongs to a gym in his neighborhood; he is also on the board of a local African American church

Social Life. Barry's friends are almost exclusively black. In the workplace, Barry is a well-regarded professional who tries to be fair minded and considerate of all his coworkers. Certainly, he doesn't see himself as prejudiced. But he will always seek out "his folks" in a formal or informal group, during lunch, or in the hallway.

Sources of News/Information/Entertainment. Barry reads the *Washington Post* and watches CNN, but he also subscribes to Afrocentric magazines and tunes in to radio and television programming that caters to black professionals.

As I said earlier, the Circle of Inclusion Zone is about your preference on a particular affiliation or value. What if you could totally control who comes into your environment? Consider how widely you would choose to cast your net. Look honestly at how much you thrive on differences. If political affiliation is a high priority, for example, do you merely tolerate members of the opposite party, or do you eagerly seek them out, happy to engage in lively debate and consider alternate perspectives?

Exercise: Charting Your Circle of Inclusion

Before you chart your Circle of Inclusion Zone, think about the following five indicators with respect to your chosen "A" affiliation or "A" value. The more questions you answer yes to, the closer you are to the closed end of the continuum.

Neighborhood/Community. Do you live in a neighborhood with people who mostly share this affiliation/value?

Critical Service Providers. Do most of your service providers (doctors, lawyers, accountants, shopkeepers, business owners, etc.) share your affiliation/value? Do you actively seek them out because of this commonality?

Membership in Social Organizations. Do you feel most comfortable in groups with people who share your affiliation/value?

Social Life. Do most of your friends share your affiliation/value? Do all of your closest friends share your affiliation/value?

Sources of News/Information/Entertainment. Do you read magazines, newspapers, or journals that are primarily targeted to your affiliation/value? What about books and movies?

Again, ask yourself as many questions as you need to accurately identify your place on the circle continuum. Now you are ready to chart your Circle of Inclusion Zone. Color in the chart below to indicate your Circle of Inclusion Zone on your chosen "A" affiliation or "A" value.

ZONE: CIRCLE OF INCLUSION
AFFILIATION: _____

Circle of Inclusion	Closed	Selective	Open

ZONE: CIRCLE OF INCLUSION
VALUE: _____

Circle of Inclusion	Closed	Selective	Open

Circle of Inclusion Implications

As you already know, each part of the zone continuum has strengths and weaknesses. With the Circle of Inclusion Zone, we are not trying to determine if you are prejudiced. There's no shame in admitting that we feel more comfortable around people with whom we have things in common. Remember, there are strengths and weaknesses at each end of the circle continuum. Your challenge is to operate out of the strengths, not the weaknesses.

For example, a weakness of the closed perspective is that you may tend to rely on preconceived notions about people who are different, rather than gaining true knowledge about them. A weakness of the open perspective is that you may tend to ignore important differences, overlooking the real problems that occur when people of conflicting views get together. Review the lists below to familiarize yourself with some of the behaviors related to the strengths and weaknesses across the zone continuum.

Zone 2: Circle of Inclusion Closed Strengths	Zone 2: Circle of Inclusion Closed Weaknesses
• Expressing pride and solidarity • Supporting those inside the circle • Reinforcing shared values • Strengthening community • Preserving traditions/beliefs • Protecting core values • Insulating yourself from bias and stereotypes	• Illegally excluding others • Closed-minded • Prejudiced/biased • Self-limiting/isolating • Rigid/lack of flexibility • Superior/elitist attitude • Maintaining purity at all cost • Living in the past • Not prepared to live and work in a multiworld

Zone 2: Circle of Inclusion Selective Strengths	Zone 2: Circle of Inclusion Selective Weaknesses
• A possible bridge to others • Broader perspective • Choosing relationships based on individual circumstances • Open to some change, but holding onto core identity	• Forcing those you let in to assimilate • Limited information • Narrow perspective

Zone 2: Circle of Inclusion Open Strengths	Zone 2: Circle of Inclusion Open Weaknesses
• Give everyone a chance • Broad-minded • Harmonizing • Optimistic about others • Curious about others • A variety of sources of information • Bridging differences • Leveraging differences • Inspirational to others	• Naive about real problems • Assuming everyone will "just get along" • Hard to find core values and beliefs • Discounting people's needs to bond with those like themselves • Trying to force yourself in where you're not wanted

Circle of Inclusion measures how we might limit our social circle to those who share our affiliations—or how open we are to including others. In this excerpt from our national survey, notice how different people measured race across the Circle of Inclusion Zone.

ZONE: CIRCLE OF INCLUSION
AFFILIATION: RACE

	White	African American	Hispanic	Asian
Closed	11.1%	32.7%	41.0%	25.2%
Selective	28.3%	28.6%	38.1%	66.9%
Open	60.6%	38.7%	20.9%	7.9%

Source: Zogby Survey
03/15/04—03/22/04
Margin of Error: +/–3.1%

6

The Commitment Zone

When F. Scott Fitzgerald said, "action is character," he was talking about the fictional characters in books. But even if you're not the tragic hero of a novel, your actions reveal a great deal about your identity. In the Commitment Zone, we'll start looking at another aspect of your identity: your depth of commitment to your affiliations and values, measured by your need to take action or create change. Commitment reveals the sensitivities that you are willing to invest capital in. By capital I mean time, money, energy, reputation, acceptance, and—in some cases—even your personal safety. The degree of commitment tells you how willing you are to be an advocate, to change the hearts and minds of others relative to your affiliations and values.

While temperature focuses on feelings, commitment focuses on behavior. For example, you may like certain politicians because they share your religion, or because they have a reputation for honesty. But do you actively get involved in their campaigns? If you think immigrant children who do not speak the local language are denied opportunities in your local schools, do you volunteer in an ESL program or organize a parent-teacher summit? Are you:

- Activist (very committed to change)
- Engaged (somewhat committed to change)
- Passive (not committed to change)

Commitment is important because it furthers defines the nature of our relationship to our affiliations and values. Whether or not we choose to act has an impact on our self-image and our relationship to the world. Take my mother, for example. There's no doubt in my mind that my mother would be considered "hot" on marital status. Since the death of my father, she has become increasingly sensitive about being a widow. She is acutely aware of her interaction in social situations now that she is no longer part of a couple. She often feels slighted or taken advantage of by repair workers, restaurant waiters, and the sales associates at department stores. But she won't speak up when she encounters social discrimination. She doesn't file complaints or demand to speak to the manager at stores. She hasn't joined a support group for widows. My mother happens to be very activist about other issues, but on this one she's passive, perhaps due to the social expectations of her generation and her region of the country, the South. (We'll talk more about how history and life experience contributes to identity zones in chapter 10.)

My mother isn't an activist, but she's still hot. The anger and resentment over perceived discrimination are real. Don't look for her handing out leaflets or standing on the picket line. But don't be surprised if she takes private action—avoiding shopping at Macy's, giving waiters lousy tips without explaining why. Picture a person like my mother, passive on an affiliation such as gender or race or age in the workplace, an office or a factory, for example. That employee may passively disengage from her job because she's stuck in a system that, to her, seems unjust. If you cannot pick up on her subtle cues, then you may learn too late, when she has taken legal action against your company, or when she has quietly retired, taking her knowledge and skill with her. A passive person still has zots, and triggering zots is always risky.

Commitment Indicators

The indicators for commitment are:

- Speaking Up
- Joining/Bonding
- Donating/Volunteering
- Advocacy/Spreading the Word
- Voting/Political Involvement

Let's use the indicators to compare the passive end of the continuum with the activist one. On the passive end, we'll look at my mother. For the activist, I'll use Jerry, the man who is hot on the value of service and concerned for the children in his community. In addition to being hot, Jerry has a high degree of commitment about this value, believing we all must contribute our time and energy toward helping others. If we compare my mother and Jerry side by side, the contrasts are stark and telling.

JERRY
VALUE: SERVICE

Temperature	Hot	Warm	Cold
Commitment	Activist	Engaged	Passive

MOTHER
AFFILIATION: MARITAL STATUS

Temperature	Hot	Warm	Cold
Commitment	Activist	Engaged	Passive

My Mother/Marital Status	*Jerry/Service*
• **Speaking Up.** My mother doesn't speak up in the moment when she feels neglected, discounted, or discriminated against because she's a widow. She doesn't voice her concerns in order to affect change.	• **Speaking Up.** Jerry believes in "giving back." He speaks up in defense of his local community. He will praise or criticize local leaders, businesses, and organizations based on whether they demonstrate a sense of compassion and commitment to those in need.
• **Joining/Bonding.** She doesn't belong to support groups for widows or other affiliated organizations (such as groups that protect the rights of elders, or groups for grieving survivors). She has some friends who are widows, but she hasn't gone out of her way to bond with other women in her situation.	• **Joining/Bonding.** He belongs to civic and service organizations. He serves on local boards and committees. He has a network of friends and contacts who place a high priority on service.
• **Donating/Volunteering.** She doesn't commit time or money toward supporting widows.	• **Donating/Volunteering.** He donates time and money to local charities, giving up many evenings and weekends.
• **Advocacy/ Spreading the Word.** She shares her feelings with a select group of individuals, but she doesn't make an effort to advocate change on behalf of the widow community.	• **Advocacy/Spreading the Word.** He recruits others in his church and his community for donations, volunteering, and other support to worthy causes. He "puts the word out" when something needs to get done.
• **Voting/Political Involvement.** She would probably vote in favor of laws that benefit widows (such as tax laws), but she wouldn't engage in a "get out the vote" campaign or actively seek change.	• **Voting/Political Involvement.** Jerry works actively for candidates who will protect the interests of the less-privileged members of the community. He contacts elected representatives to voice his approval or disapproval at their public positions in relation to local issues.

Exercise: Charting Your Commitment

Are you activist, engaged or passive, or somewhere in between? Before you chart your commitment, think about the following five indicators with respect to your chosen "A" affiliation or "A" value. Once again, answering "yes" places you farther toward the left (activist) side of the continuum.

Speaking Up. Do you speak up for people who share your value/affiliation if they are slighted or discounted?

Joining/Bonding. Do you join groups that support/empower people who share your value/affiliation? Do you feel a special bond with other people who share your value/affiliation?

Donating/Volunteering. Do you donate time or money to causes that support people who share your value/affiliation?

Advocacy/Spreading the Word. Do you advocate on behalf of others who share your value/affiliation? Will you "spread the word" when people of your value/affiliation have been helped or slighted by a person or a business?

Voting/Political Involvement. Do you vote for people because you share the same value/affiliation?

In some cases, you may have to think creatively about the indicators. For example, most people don't join "Honesty Clubs," but they do seek out friends who share their values. You cannot donate money to Honesty, Inc. But you can use honesty as one of your criteria when evaluating the organizations or individuals that deserve your time and money.

Now you are ready to chart your commitment. Color in the chart below to indicate your commitment on your chosen "A" affiliation or "A" value.

ZONE: COMMITMENT
AFFILIATION: _____

Commitment	Activist	Engaged	Passive

ZONE: COMMITMENT

VALUE: _____

Commitment	Activist	Engaged	Passive

Commitment Implications

There is no wrong place to fall within the commitment continuum, any more than there is a wrong place to fall within temperature or circle of inclusion. Your challenge is always to operate from the strengths, not the weaknesses, of your position.

If you're passive on certain affiliations and values, it's worth noting that some of "your folks"—the people who share those affiliations/values—may resent you for not taking action. This is the case for my friend Roger, a gay man I've known for many years. He will not volunteer, attend support groups or rallies, protest, hand out leaflets, canvas for gay political candidates, or join political organizations that advocate gay issues. At most, Roger will donate money to some related causes. His gay friends are appalled, but Roger is just not inspired or moved to be an activist on this issue.

If you're at the activist end of the continuum, like Roger's friends, it's valuable to keep in mind that we all choose our battles, and that not respecting an individual's choices can push away a friend and ally.

Review the lists below to familiarize yourself with some of the additional strengths and weaknesses across the commitment continuum.

Zone 3: Commitment Activist Strengths	Zone 3: Commitment Activist Weaknesses
• Earnest • Focused • Inspiring • Moral • Selfless • Generous • Community focused • Putting your money where your mouth is • Self-sacrificing • Committed	• In your face • One note/Single focus • Attacking • Blaming • Shaming • A hammer that sees everything as a nail • Them/us thinking • Black/white thinking • Lack of balance • Lacking humor • Self-righteous

Zone 3: Commitment Engaged Strengths	Zone 3: Commitment Engaged Weaknesses
• Strategic responses • Reasonable • Balanced use of energy • Able to see both perspectives • Focused attention • Resources used judiciously • Possible bridge between others	• Not willing to take risks • Hiding • Wishy-washy • Self-serving • Supporting those who are harming others

Zone 3: Commitment Passive Strengths	Zone 3: Commitment Passive Weaknesses
• Careful • Considerate • Deliberative • Not rash • Above the fray • Not harming others	• Afraid • Hiding your head in the sand • In denial • Irresponsible • Not supporting those in need

Commitment measures the level of our dedication to a specific affiliation—or how we disregard such affiliations. In this excerpt from our national survey, notice how men and women described their commitment to causes related to their gender.

ZONE: COMMITMENT
AFFILIATION: GENDER

	Male	Female
Activist	13.5%	37.2%
Engaged	34.1%	41.5%
Passive	52.4%	21.3%

Source: Zogby Survey
03/15/04–03/22/04
Margin of Error: +/–3.1%

7

The Strategy Zone

Now we move on to the fourth zone, strategy. Like the Commitment Zone, the Strategy Zone measures your actions. What kind of "actor" are you? Commitment tells us if you feel motivated to act. Strategy tells us what kinds of actions you're likely to take. By distinguishing between types of actions, the strategy zone further refines and clarifies your relationship to your affiliations and values. At one end of the strategy continuum, you are likely to go on the offensive, battling people and institutions, seeking a revolution, or radical change. At the other end, you may work within the rules of the existing institutions to slightly modify or defend the existing system.

Strategy is most easily understood as a measure of how much you are invested in the status quo. When trying to assess your strategy, think about what you are willing to do to affect change on your high-priority affiliations and values. Create an entirely new vision that calls for the dissolution of the current state? Work for gradual reformation? Work within the existing structure?

Which of these descriptions fits you best:

- **Transformational** (I believe the existing values and systems are fundamentally outmoded, dysfunctional, or corrupt and must be replaced.)
- **Reformist** (I believe in improving, reclaiming, strengthening, and/or fixing existing values and systems.)
- **Conformist** (I believe in preserving, obeying, and protecting the existing values and systems.)

To better understand strategy, let's look at someone who has strong feelings about some high-priority values but uses a conformist strategy to take action.

Kevin decided to become a vegetarian on his thirtieth birthday. An animal lover since childhood, he had always respected vegetarians, believing they had made a difficult, self-sacrificing choice. Kevin was at a point in his life where he felt pressure to make a difference—to turn his deeply held beliefs into actual, day-to-day behavior. His response to this ethical dilemma is as revealing as the beliefs themselves. How could he keep downing his much-beloved cheeseburgers when, in his heart, he believed that eating meat was wrong? It became more important to him to maintain the integrity of his beliefs than to satisfy a passing desire. He explains:

> Most people would be surprised to know that I feel so deeply about this issue. I am not a warrior or an activist for the cause. I do not make a show of my vegetarianism. If people ask me about it, I tell them the reasons for my conversion, but I have never marched in a protest or sent money to PETA (People for the Ethical Treatment of Animals). I think that moral choices are inherently private things, the by-products of careful thought and spiritual guidance. I'm not sure we can ever force people to understand our choices, let alone accept them.

Kevin's vegetarianism originates from several values. He believes human beings have a responsibility to respect and care for the natural world, including animals. He also believes that eating meat is morally wrong. Kevin prioritizes integrity and prefers to "puts his money where his mouth is," matching his beliefs to his actions. Kevin's story is a good example of the way the multiple affiliations and values can affect our choices in life. Later, we'll talk more about "stacking" or "unpacking" the dynamics of a situation when multiple affiliations and values are at play.

First, let's look at Kevin's story from the perspective of a single value, nature. Kevin charts himself as warm-hot on nature. He charts himself as engaged on the commitment scale, because he is openly vegetarian and speaks up and explains his point of view when someone questions his choice. But on strategy, Kevin tends toward the conformist end of the continuum. Kevin is not, as he readily admits, a reformer or transformer. He isn't out to change the system. He may not like the existing systems and societal norms, but he's not trying to start a revolution, advocate a new world order, or compel everyone to become vegetarian. He wouldn't lay his life on the line or break the law to get his point across.

KEVIN

Temperature	Hot	Warm	Cold
		Nature	
Circle of Inclusion	Closed	Selective	Open Nature
Commitment	Activist	Engaged Nature	Passive
Strategy	Transform	Reform	Conform Nature

Kevin's strategy is conformist regardless of his strong feelings and his impulse to act. This is true even when another value, integrity, is "stacked" on top of nature, increasing the intensity of temperature and commitment that intersect in Kevin's choice to become vegetarian.

Why is Kevin's strategy conformist? As he explains above, he sees his vegetarianism as a private moral choice. On other issues, when other affiliations and values come into play, his strategy is different, and he tends more toward the transformational end of the continuum. For some people, however, the conformist strategy is a natural tendency across all their affiliations and values. Conformist personalities prefer to work within the existing systems and laws, regardless of their temperature and commitment.

Strategy and History

Like all the identity zones, strategy is an area where we evolve and change due to our life circumstances. Many of us are conformist or reformist until something "snaps" in our lives—until a pivotal event or historical movement pushes us toward more dramatic, revolutionary thinking. Strategy plays a special role in the history of nations, because it is so often the catalyst for change. History is full of examples of mass transformational thinking and political revolution—for better or for worse. In such cases, individuals are swept up into a revolutionary fervor, sometimes by choice, sometimes by external pressure.

For example, consider two early American wars, the War of Independence and the Civil War. Both were driven by transformational strategies that took strong temperatures and strong passions and pushed them onto the battlefield. Thousands put their lives on the line. These were wars of ideology and identity, ignited by a unique combination of events, circumstances, and explosive combinations of values and affiliations. Left to their own devices, not all the soldiers who fought would have chosen a transformational course of action. But societal pressure—and the pressure of the military—swept them up into a transformational war that changed the course of history.

Sometimes a society's culture goes through a period of reform or transformation, and ordinary citizens find themselves under pressure to change their attitudes, forced to confront difficult questions about certain affiliations or values. This certainly happened during the Civil Rights era in the United States, when temperatures flared, tensions erupted, and awareness about societal injustices and inequalities swelled. By the end of the 1960s, our country was a pressure cooker on affiliations and values such as gender, race, age, political affiliation, patriotism, and morality, to name a few. Hot, activist individuals were everywhere—and for many the question wasn't whether to take action and seek change, but how far to go.

Some within our society were not only advocating a new vision, but also calling for a violent revolution. With so many transformational thinkers, degrees of difference at the transformational end of the continuum were magnified. This magnification was dramatized by two famous individuals of that era who were hot, activist, and advocating change on race: Dr. Martin Luther King, Jr. and Huey Newton of the Black Panther Party.

These two men agreed that black Americans were oppressed. They agreed that the time for change had come. But they expressed their perspectives on strategy differently, as you can see by comparing the quotes below.

> Nonviolence is the answer to the crucial political and moral questions of our time; the need for mankind to overcome oppression and violence without resorting to oppression and violence. Mankind must evolve for all human conflict a method that rejects revenge, aggression, and retaliation. The foundation of such a method is love.
>
> Dr. Martin Luther King, Jr.,

> We realize that it's they who are criminals and it's they who will have to be brought to justice. We will have to go on fighting in spite of the losses and in spite of the hardships that we're bound to suffer, until the final downfall of the reactionary power structure.
>
> Huey P. Newton
> Minister of Defense, Black Panther Party

Martin Luther King rallied millions of people. He raised awareness about racial injustice and used civil disobedience as a tool for change, bringing an end to the era of unfair laws and "acceptable" intolerance. He was willing to break the law and pay the consequences under the law in a symbolic act to reform the existing system.

By contrast, Huey Newton and the Black Panthers wanted to get rid of the laws. They believed the entire reactionary power structure had to go. The system was corrupt, beyond repair, and Newton considered himself an officer in a new power structure—a warrior using extreme tactics. With a wartime mentality, the Black Panthers were not only willing to put their lives on the line; they used violence in the name of justice.

Today, of course, the Civil Rights era has given way to the era of diversity and multiculturalism. There are still people whose strategy on race is transformational, and they may experience conflicts among themselves about degrees of transformation. But the more compelling contrast on race in our country today is typified by reformist-transformational versus conformist-reformist strategies. Think about Supreme Court Justice Clarence Thomas, for example, a man whose investment in the status quo is best expressed by this opinion on the American constitution:

Of course, even when strictly interpreted as I believe it should be, the Constitution remains a modern, "breathing" document as some like to call it, in the strict sense that the Court is constantly required to interpret how its provisions apply to the Constitutional questions of modern life. Nevertheless, strict interpretation must never surrender to the understandably attractive impulse towards creative but unwarranted alterations of first principles.

Clarence Thomas
Supreme Court Justice
February 15, 2001

Strategy Indicators

The indicators for strategy are:

- New Societal Vision
- Breakthrough Concepts/Ideas
- Revolutionary Thinking
- Willingness to Do Battle/Go to War
- Sense of Urgency
- Belief That the End Justifies the Means

To show how these indicators apply to strategy, we'll use the example of Kevin and his strategy on nature, integrity and vegetarianism.

New Societal Vision. Kevin has personal vision, not a societal vision. When he chose the vegetarian lifestyle, he didn't expect the rest of the world to follow suit.

Breakthrough Concepts/Ideas. Kevin had no interest in pursuing new ideas about being vegetarian, preserving the natural world, or acting with integrity. Because his choice was simple—eating meat versus not eating meat—he took a conventional approach to solving his ethical problem.

Revolutionary Thinking. Kevin did not want to start a vegetarian revolution; he didn't want to punish meat eaters, change laws, or write new laws to protect animals.

Willingness to Do Battle/Go to War. Kevin was not interested in taking up arms, either figuratively or literally. He didn't see the issue as an "us versus them" battle—and he certainly would never take violent action to protest meat eating.

Sense of Urgency. Although a staunch proponent of resource management, Kevin saw no immediate, catastrophic consequences if people continued to eat meat; in fact, since he had only recently converted to this lifestyle, he did not feel comfortable preaching to others about it.

Belief that the End Justifies the Means. Kevin would not take dangerous or violent actions (such as threats, vandalism, bombings, kidnappings, etc.) to further the vegetarian cause.

Exercise: Charting Your Strategy

Before you chart your strategy, think about the following indicators with respect to your chosen "A" affiliation or "A" value. Are you transformational, believing the existing values and systems are fundamentally outmoded, dysfunctional, or corrupt and must be replaced? Reformist: believing in improving, reclaiming, strengthening, and/or fixing existing values and systems? Or conformist: believing in preserving, obeying, and protecting the existing values and systems? As always, the more you answer yes to the questions, the more you belong on the left (transformational) end of the continuum.

New Societal Vision. Do you advocate a new vision or system that is fundamentally different from the current system? Will it affect everyone, not just those who share your affiliation/value?

Breakthrough Concepts/Ideas. Do you have a new idea you believe will revolutionize the way we think about the world in relation to your affiliation/value?

Revolutionary Thinking. Are you advocating the forceful overthrow of the existing system, values, and norms related to your affiliation/value?

Willingness to Do Battle/Go to War. Do you see changing the system as an "us versus them" battle? Are you willing to go to war or take physical action to ensure justice and fairness related to your affiliation/value?

Sense of Urgency. Do you feel time is running out? Do you feel the situation is so dire, the consequences so terrible, that urgent action is needed to change things related to your affiliation/value?

Belief That the End Justifies the Means. Do you believe that it is acceptable to "do whatever it takes" in order to change the current system, values and norms?

Now you are ready to chart your strategy. Color in the chart below to indicate your strategy on your chosen "A" affiliation or "A" value.

ZONE 4: STRATEGY
AFFILIATION: _____

Strategy	Transform	Reform	Conform

ZONE 4: STRATEGY
VALUE: _____

Strategy	Transform	Reform	Conform

Strategy Implications

Why is strategy important? Yesterday I picked up the newspaper and read about a young Palestinian woman, a so-called suicide bomber who killed herself and four Israelis. She left her two children motherless and her husband a widower. Her story was a reminder that the Strategy Zone can have life-or-death consequences. As I sit here, safely sequestered in my house in suburban Maryland, tragic conflicts are brewing around the world, destroying individual lives, families, communities, and countries.

It can be hard to understand why someone takes drastic measures. But I think we must try. Without sensitivity and understanding, how can the global community help resolve conflict? How can we turn the dream of world peace into reality? The young Palestinian woman believed in paying any price to defend her religion and her country, even sacrificing the lives of others.

At one extreme of the strategy continuum, a transformational strategy is drastic, violent, even deadly. In most cases it arises from a desperate sense of fear, urgency, anger, injustice—a powerful brew of emotions that we've all experienced on some level in our lives. As you review the implications across the strategy continuum, imagine a scenario in which you have to defend yourself against an enemy—someone trying to deprive you of everything that matters most. Try, if you can, to understand what it's like to feel threatened to the core. Maybe you've felt that way in the past, or you feel that way now. Maybe you will feel that way in the future.

Both ends of the strategy continuum have weaknesses as well as strengths. A conformist strategy misses opportunities for essential growth and change. Where would we be without people like Gandhi, Martin Luther King, Helen Keller? Yet when we tend toward the transformational, we risk profound consequences for individuals, communities and nations. Operating out of the strengths, not the weaknesses, is a challenge that we all share as members of the global community.

Zone 4: Strategy Transform Strengths	Zone 4: Strategy Transform Weaknesses
• Visionary • Breakthrough thinking • Unyielding • Missionary • Savior-Martyr • Warrior/Liberator/Freedom fighter • Courageous	• Unrealistic • Violent • Myopic/no shared vision • Not honoring where people are • Inhumane • Irrational • Impatient/Rushing/Moving too fast • Destroyer-Martyr • Terrorist

Zone 4: Strategy Reform Strengths	Zone 4: Strategy Reform Weaknesses
• Working within the system • Not throwing baby out with bathwater • Acting as a bridge between others • Mediator • Pride and investment in the system	• Wait too late to respond • Suggest changes that are not significant enough to address the problem • Misread the degree of dissatisfaction that others feel

Zone 4: Strategy Conform Strengths	Zone 4: Strategy Conform Weaknesses
• Obeying the laws, rules, and norms adding to stability • Preserve, protect, and defend the status quo • Acceptance and credibility within the status quo	• Protecting parts of the system that no longer work • Completely out of touch with the negative impact of aspects of the status quo on others • Stuck in the past, afraid and unwilling to accept necessary change

Strategy measures how we work within—or without—existing systems and institutions to effectively advocate change for an affiliation. In this excerpt from our national survey, notice how respondents in different industries described their strategy when it comes to line of work.

ZONE: STRATEGY
AFFILIATION: PROFESSION

	Blue Collar	Homemaker	Managerial	Sales	Clerical
Transform	47.1%	30.1%	21.8%	13.6%	9.2%
Reform	13.5%	27.0%	20.5%	19.0%	13.5%
Conform	39.4%	42.8%	57.7%	67.4%	77.3%

Source: Zogby Survey
03/15/04—03/22/04
Margin of Error: +/–3.1%

8

The Power Zone

No one can make you feel inferior without your consent.

—Eleanor Roosevelt, *This Is My Story*

The Power Zone is the fifth zone, the final zone we're going to discuss in this part of the book. To put the Power Zone in the proper context, let's take a moment to recap the identity zones we've discussed already.

- **Temperature** is about sensitivity.
- **Circle of Inclusion** is about who you choose to associate with.
- **Commitment** is about your willingness to take action and create change.
- **Strategy** is about how you create change.

How does *power* fit into the Identity Zones framework? The Power Zone measures how capable you feel of controlling your destiny with respect to your affiliations and values. It measures how you gauge your ability to harness and deploy the personal, situational, and societal assets at your disposal to create the outcome you desire—whether in your home, workplace, community, or society.

For example, do you feel like your socioeconomic status is preventing you from reaching your professional goals, or do you feel capable of pulling yourself up by the bootstraps regardless of obstacles? On the value of world peace, do you believe your power of persuasion is so great that you can win hearts and minds around the globe, or do you feel powerless in the face of centuries of cyclical war, conflicting ideologies, and the complexities of international relations?

The Power Zone is not an objective measure of your control over others. The Power Zone is about your *perceived power*. We use the Power Zone to figure out how confident you feel, because your self-perception affects how your zots get triggered and what happens when they do. What is your perceived level of power?

- **High** (highly capable and effective)
- **Medium** (moderately capable and effective)
- **Low** (ineffective in the face of obstacles/individuals)

The Power Zone tends to be highly contextual. It not only changes over time; it also changes interaction by interaction, situation by situation. But just because power is less "fixed" than the other zones doesn't make it less important. If we overlook power, we may misread the other zones. What if someone is a hot activist but feels completely powerless due to circumstances beyond his or her control? What if an authority figure—a boss, a parent—is the one triggering your zots? We'll discuss the dynamics of power more in "Reading Relationships," part 3 of the book. For now, let's move on to an example of the way power influences our attitudes and choices.

Carla is a partner in a small consulting company, a professional in her mid-forties with a degree from a technical college. She is proud of her achievements in the workplace and confident in her ability to work diligently, apply her intelligence, and make decisions. Carla is also a wife and devoted mother; she doesn't see herself as a stereotypical feminist.

One of Carla's zots was recently triggered by an offhand comment. During a phone conference, a senior executive named Joe called her a girl. Feeling insulted and angry, Carla faced a moment of truth: should she ignore the insult or speak up? She chose to act, questioning the executive on his use of the term. She explained that it was inappropriate, a personally and professionally trivializing comment. Carla guessed that

he had probably insulted other women in the past, but they were too intimidated to protest.

Here's what Carla has to say about the results of her interaction with Joe:

> From that point on, he has not referred to me as a *girl*. Occasionally he slips
> and uses *girl* or *girls*, but he quickly apologizes and says *woman* or *women*
> instead. He told me on the phone recently that he was in a board meeting
> and used the term *woman*. Several men and women teased him for being
> politically correct—apparently, they were used to the old Joe and unsure
> what to make of the change. Even though his colleagues teased him, I am
> sure that the women in the room appreciated not being called *girls*.

The chart below shows Carla's temperature, commitment, strategy,
and power on gender. In her interaction with Joe, Carla felt empowered
to act on her other zones. She felt capable of speaking up and making a
difference when she felt disrespected as a woman. In this context—a
business meeting—Carla rated her power at the medium-high end of
the power continuum.

CARLA
AFFILIATION: GENDER

Temperature	Hot	Warm	Cold
Circle of Inclusion	Closed	Selective	Open
Commitment	Activist	Engaged	Passive
Strategy	Transform	Reform	Conform
Power	High	Medium	Low

Power Indicators

In today's society we talk a lot about empowerment. To feel empowered
is to feel free of past constraints, to feel strong and capable of controlling one's own path in life. This is different from the kind of power held
by dictators or CEOs or parents—power that is purely about control
and authority. There are lots of reasons why people feel powerful.
Sometimes we feel powerful because we're confident, charismatic, well
educated, and articulate, or because we have professional credentials

and good reputations, or because the law is on our side, or because we have friends, allies, money, social standing, seniority, an impressive title . . . the list goes on and on. I think it's useful to break power into three categories:

Personal Power. Charisma, talent, intellect, self-confidence, determination, and persuasiveness

Situational/Hierarchal Power. Organizational rank or title, money, knowledge, resources, status, majority rule

Societal Power. Social norms, ethics, and laws

These categories aren't neat and tidy, but they help put different kinds of power in context. As you start thinking about your place on the power continuum, you can use these as indicators to diagnose your power more accurately. Your place on the zone continuum (high, medium, or low) is determined by assessing your perceived power on each.

Let's assess the Carla/Joe conflict according to these three indicators.

Personal Power. I described Carla at the beginning of the chapter as "confident in her ability to work diligently, apply her intelligence, and make decisions." She sees herself as a powerful woman who deserves respect and knows how to get it, especially at this stage in her career. Thus, her perceived personal power is high.

Situational/Hierarchal Power. Joe is a senior-level executive with access to money, resources, and powerful people. He outranks Carla in the organization and holds more sway in the business world. But Carla's senior management position (as partner) gave her a high degree of relative power—compared to, say, an administrative assistant. Her perceived situational/hierarchal power is medium.

Societal Power. Carla felt empowered to address this issue because societal norms and expectations have made Joe's use of the word girl—especially in the workplace—unacceptable. These societal norms and expectations are based, in part, on laws that protect women from discrimination and from hostile work environments. We may not have achieved total gender equity in the workplace, but society has come to a general consensus about discrimination and disrespect. Carla's perceived societal power is somewhere between medium and high.

Exercise: Charting Your Power

Before you chart your power, think about the following three indicators with respect to your chosen "A" affiliation or "A" value. Your answers to these questions will help you place yourself on the power continuum. For an accurate assessment, you may wish to use a specific situation, interaction, or relationship to judge your power in context.

Personal Power. How influential and effective are you in communicating your needs and sensitivities related to your affiliation/value? Are you so charismatic or convincing that you can compel people to change their behavior?

Situational/Hierarchal Power. Do you have a high degree of official power, organizational power, or physical/psychological control related to your affiliation/value?

Societal Power. Do the societal norms, customs, traditions, and/or laws protect you based on your affiliation/value?

Now you are ready to chart your power. Color in the chart below to indicate your power on your chosen "A" affiliation or "A" value.

ZONE 5: POWER
AFFILIATION: _____

Power	High	Medium	Low

ZONE 5: POWER
VALUE: _____

Power	High	Medium	Low

Power Implications

Developing an awareness of your perceived power is essential, because the consequences of misreading a situation may be very negative indeed. It's important to understand that sometimes you actually have more power than you think. It's also important to remember that some relationships and situations have an inherent imbalance of power that dramatically changes the dynamics.

What if Joe had called someone other than Carla a girl—someone who didn't think she had the power to confront him? If Carla had been an administrative assistant, perhaps the conversation never would have happened. Have you ever wanted to speak up in a meeting, but the person on the other side of the table was more senior or worked in a more powerful part of the organization? If you did speak up, would you have had any allies or supporters? Perhaps someone in your home or your community triggered a zot, but you purposely chose not to act because you felt intimidated or ineffectual.

Again, take a look at the lists below to familiarize yourself with some of the strengths and weaknesses of part of the power continuum. If you think of additional strengths or weaknesses, you can add them.

Zone 5: Power High Strengths	Zone 5: Power High Weaknesses
• Leverage your power • Act as a stakeholder • Drive change or preserve status quo • Serve/support others • Keep others in line • Marshal and deploy resources • Shape opinion • Actualize your vision	• Arrogant • Manipulate others • Exploit others • Develop a cult following • Create/change rules to fit your desired outcome • See others as pawns • Disregard others' needs, feelings, and rights

Zone 5: Power Medium Strengths	Zone 5: Power Medium Weaknesses
• Join others, consolidate power • Advocate for your position • Can support and nurture those who have less power • Can influence those who have more power	• Because of fear you don't utilize the power you have

Zone 5: Power Low Strengths	Zone 5: Power Low Weaknesses
• Spiritual awareness of suffering • Drawing support from higher or inner power • More attuned and aware of others' suffering • Joining together with others to make a difference • Accepting support and resources from others • Able to form moral arguments	• Playing the victim • Looking for handouts • Waiting to be saved • Blaming others • Dependent • Lack of self-respect • Guilt-inducing • Afraid to stand up for self • Stuck

Power measures how we feel about our ability to control day-to-day issues related to an affiliation—or how we may feel powerless to do so. In this excerpt from our national survey, notice how respondents from different parties described their power when it comes to political affiliation.

ZONE: POWER
AFFILIATION: POLITICAL AFFILIATION

	Republican	Democrat	Independent/ Minor
High	17.8%	12.9%	3.6%
Medium	16.7%	20.5%	25.0%
Low	65.7%	66.6%	71.3%

Source: Zogby Survey
03/15/04–03/22/04
Margin of Error: +/–3.1%

9

Building a
Full Portrait

U p to this point, we've been building your Identity Zones chart zone by zone, deepening your understanding of a single affiliation or value in each chapter. Now it's time to stand back and see the bigger picture. What are the key aspects of your identity? Which patterns do you see emerging through your Identity Zones? Building a full portrait helps you take the next step toward knowing yourself, pinpointing potential zots, and concentrating on operating out of your zone strengths. With the Identity Zones framework, patterns or tendencies can emerge on a single affiliation/value, or on multiple affiliations/values.

Stacking and Unpacking

To begin, let's take a look at the chart you've completed already. Go back and refresh your memory about where you fall within each zone continuum on your chosen affiliation/value. Use this table to shade all of the placements that you made within the previous zones.

AFFILIATION/VALUE: _____

Temperature	Hot	Warm	Cold
Circle of Inclusion	Closed	Selective	Open
Commitment	Activist	Engaged	Passive
Strategy	Transform	Reform	Conform
Power	High	Medium	Low

To understand stacking and unpacking, try to picture the chart above as part of a 3-D model. You have a series of five *zones* you've filled out from top to bottom, and *continuums* you've filled out from left to right. Thus far you've been working in these two dimensions of the Identity Zones framework. What's the third? *Multiple* affiliations and values. Remember, this chart represents only a single value/affiliation. Imagine stacking additional charts on top of the chart above. For example, if this is a chart of your professional affiliation, imagine stacking additional charts on affiliations such as:

- Race
- Gender
- Regional Affiliation

Now imagine stacking even more charts on values such as:

- Honesty
- Integrity
- Professionalism
- Leisure/Fun

This is what I mean by stacking: building a full portrait by adding additional affiliations and values, one on top of another, to search for patterns and potential zots. *Unpacking* is doing this in reverse, analyzing a situation or relationship by taking the stacks of affiliations and values apart.

Heat Waves and Cold Fronts

When you're stacking and unpacking, one of the patterns to look for is a tendency to fall toward the left (hot) or right (cold) side of the identity zones chart.

If you tend to run hot, you may be a hot personality, or *heat wave*.

If you tend to run cold, you may be a cold personality, or *cold front*.

Multiple affiliations or values on the hot side, particularly in temperature, intensify your reactions; those on the cold side do the opposite. In either case, you need to be aware of your actions and reactions in order to build and maintain successful relationships.

Olivia: The Story of a Heat Wave

I'm going to give you some examples now that illustrate how stacking can give us a fuller portrait of an individual. We'll begin with my friend and colleague Olivia.

I have known Olivia for more than twenty years. She is a brilliant consultant, educator, community activist, and dear friend. She helped teach me how to laugh, how to look at issues soulfully, and how to act with real integrity. But Olivia is also a challenging friend because she has lots of zots. Trigger a zot on Olivia, and you can count on an indignant, passionate response.

A few years ago, Olivia and I were working together as consultants, helping a client with team issues in the workplace. To illustrate a point about marital and parental status, I drew a diagram showing the many different combinations of people that make up the modern workforce. I placed each category on a chart: married with children, married without children, divorced parents, single parents. To indicate people who didn't fit either category—single, unmarried, childless—I placed a zero on the chart.

Olivia happened to fall into the last category—single, unmarried, without children. At the next break, she really let me have it. She saw my zero as an assault on her, because she felt that society tends to treat women of her age "as a zero" if they don't have children. We didn't have time to hash this out, so I chuckled a bit and asked if she was serious. This made matters worse. Olivia was extremely hot on the combination of stacked affiliations in this situation: marital status, parental status, and age. My response was inflammatory, and she was furious.

Let's first look at Olivia's Identity Zones chart on a single affiliation: parental status. As you can see below, Olivia is not all the way over to the hot side of the continuum in every zone. Olivia is not a political or public advocate for parental issues; she will not fight to preserve or enhance the rights of childless workers. She will not try to reform the current system on this issue. She just wants more sensitivity and support for women who do not have children. Olivia does not have the ability to control all of the societal norms and expectations related to having children, but she does have a great deal of personal power, and she can't be discriminated against by law.

OLIVIA
AFFILIATION: PARENTAL STATUS

Temperature	Hot	Warm	Cold
	Parental Status		
Circle of Inclusion	Closed	Selective	Open
		Parental Status	
Commitment	Activist	Engaged	Passive
		Parental Status	
Strategy	Transform	Reform	Conform
			Parental Status
Power	High	Medium	Low
		Parental Status	

On parental status, Olivia is not clustered at the left side of the continuum. So why is Olivia a heat wave? Because she is hot on multiple affiliations and values. Stacking them reveals a heat wave personality. Let me tell you another story. Several weeks after the "zero" blowout, I celebrated my thirty-fifth birthday. My wife had planned a steak dinner and I asked Olivia to join us. Olivia seemed delighted by the invitation, but then asked who else was coming. I went through the list of invitees.

"Hmmm, all married couples," Olivia said. She preferred to reschedule some other time with me alone, because she felt left out in couples-only situations and consciously tried to avoid them. I responded with disregard for another one of her zots: marital status.

"Oh, come on," I said. "You must be kidding. This is my birthday we're talking about."

"This is my life we're talking about!" she said.

Olivia is hot on marital status. She is very selective about interacting with people who are married or coupled—she prefers to spend time with single people. This issue personally engages her, and she demands sensitivity and respect. But (as with the parental affiliation) she is not trying to reform or transform the institution of marriage as we know it. Olivia has some personal power to influence how she is treated as a single woman, but her power is limited by a powerful legacy of societal norms. Think about a word like "spinster," no longer "PC," but still potent in a society where marriage and childbearing are expected of women.

OLIVIA
AFFILIATION: MARITAL STATUS

Temperature	Hot	Warm	Cold
	Marital Status		
Circle of Inclusion	Closed	Selective	Open
		Marital Status	
Commitment	Activist	Engaged	Passive
		Marital Status	
Strategy	Transform	Reform	Conform
			Marital Status
Power	High	Medium	Low
		Marital Status	

Let's share one more story about Olivia. She once went on a date with a man, only to discover during the evening that he belonged to a different political party than she did. Of course, they did not see political issues eye to eye, and Olivia's zots were triggered numerous times during the date. Olivia told me later that if she'd known about his beliefs, she would never have gone out with him. She said she refuses to date anyone whom she considers politically misguided and out of touch. When Olivia asked me for validation on this perspective, I asked her (yet again) if she was kidding: wasn't she throwing the baby out with the bathwater? Wrong response. Olivia was not amused.

Olivia is also closed on political affiliation. This means that she prefers to socialize and form bonds with people who share her political perspective. She volunteers for political campaigns and makes significant contributions to the candidate of her choice. As the visionary leader of her organization, Olivia works closely with elected officials to change the power dynamic within communities. Thus, she has very high personal power; her situational power is also high because she commands human and financial and resources.

OLIVIA
AFFILIATION: POLITICAL

Temperature	Hot Political Affiliation	Warm	Cold
Circle of Inclusion	Closed Political Affiliation	Selective	Open
Commitment	Activist Political Affiliation	Engaged	Passive
Strategy	Transform Political Affiliation	Reform	Conform
Power	High Political Affiliation	Medium	Low

Below, I've stacked all three of Olivia's charts to create a fuller portrait. When we stack three of her high-priority affiliations—parental status, marital status, and political affiliation—we wind up with a lot of heat! If you're a heat wave personality, like my friend Olivia, your unyielding passion and dedication may be a pain sometimes. But you help keep the rest of us honest. Managing a successful relationship with you is both difficult and necessary.

OLIVIA
AFFILIATIONS: PARENTAL, POLITICAL, MARITAL

Temperature	Hot Parental Status Political Affiliation Marital Status	Warm	Cold
Circle of Inclusion	Closed Political Affiliation	Selective Parental Status Marital Status	Open
Commitment	Activist Political Affiliation	Engaged Parental Status Marital Status	Passive
Strategy	Transform Political Affiliation	Reform	Conform Parental Status Marital Status
Power	High	Medium Parental Status Marital Status	Low
		Political Affiliation	

Greg and Alejandro: Stacking and Conflict

I once worked with a communications company that had an intern program. Midlevel managers were paired with interns (high school students) and asked to nurture them along, teaching them about the informal norms of working within an organization. Many managers were uncomfortable with the idea, because they were nervous about cross-cultural interaction. Greg, a forty-five-year-old white man with a college degree from the Midwest, was assigned to mentor Alejandro, a seventeen-year-old Mexican American from the inner city. Let's compare Greg and Alejandro on two affiliations: race and age.

Greg: Race

Greg was uncomfortable with Alejandro; in fact, he was uncomfortable with the whole idea of the mentoring program. Greg was cold on the affiliation of race. He rarely thought about the fact that he was white. He had little passion for issues related to race or ethnicity, and he was comfortable maintaining the status quo, which he saw as fair and merit-based. He also placed a high value on self-reliance and professionalism. Was this young man being given a special opportunity just because he was Hispanic? Greg didn't know much about Hispanic culture. Most of Greg's friends were white, so he couldn't fill in the blanks. If it were up to Greg, he would never have established a mentoring program in the first place. But it wasn't up to him, and he was annoyed by his sense of low power.

GREG
AFFILIATION: RACE

Temperature	Hot	Warm	Cold
			Race
Circle of Inclusion	Closed	Selective	Open
	Race		
Commitment	Activist	Engaged	Passive
			Race
Strategy	Transform	Reform	Conform
			Race
Power	High	Medium	Low
			Race

Greg: Age

Greg was also uncomfortable with the age gap between him and his mentee. Alejandro ended his screening interview with a burst of idiomatic dialogue, saying something about the job being "fresh" and "smacking." Greg had no idea what he meant. At forty-five and in the "sweet spot" of his career, Greg had proven that he was mature enough to handle most challenging assignments. He still had future potential and was far from being called over the hill. He lived in a suburban community largely populated by other successful, middle-aged, career-oriented people. He rarely had to interact with young urban teens. Greg encountered no intolerance about his age and enjoyed the benefits that the society bestows on professional men of a certain age generation. He had the power to control most of the issues related to his age: health care decisions, schools for his young children, supporting his aging parents, and so on.

GREG
AFFILIATION: AGE

Temperature	Hot	Warm	Cold
			Age
Circle of Inclusion	Closed	Selective	Open
	Age		
Commitment	Activist	Engaged	Passive
			Age
Strategy	Transform	Reform	Conform
			Age
Power	High	Medium	Low
	Age		

Alejandro: Race

Alejandro was very proud of his Latin heritage and sensitive about how he and other Latinos are perceived and treated. He lived in a community with other Latinos. His family was politically active, supporting a range of political and social empowerment issues related to their Mexican American community. Alejandro was only interested in the internship because it offered him some exposure to publishing techniques. He wanted to put this experience to work for a progressive (some would say "radical") community newspaper. Alejandro saw his overall power as low to moderate, because so many social norms related to race and ethnicity were negative, based on his cultural experience. But he wielded a great deal of personal influence over other students and those within his community. He was considered an important role model and youth leader.

ALEJANDRO
AFFILIATION: RACE

Temperature	Hot	Warm	Cold
	Race		
Circle of Inclusion	Closed	Selective	Open
	Race		
Commitment	Activist	Engaged	Passive
	Race		
Strategy	Transform	Reform	Conform
	Race		
Power	High	Medium	Low
			Race

Alejandro: Age

Alejandro was hypersensitive about his age. He was tired of being told what he could and could not do, tired of having older people make all the key decisions on his behalf, and tired of their assumptions about his capabilities and maturity. His friends were more like him, and he preferred to be with his peer group. He was always trying to change the rules-related age requirements in order to participate in adult activities. For example, the internship program itself was restricted to those eighteen and older. Alejandro and his fellow students successfully circulated and submitted a petition to allow seventeen-year-olds in. In this situation, Alejandro worked with the system to create the reform that he wanted. While he is seen within his peer group as a leader (and by some adults as a role model), he still feels that the society is unfairly limiting and intolerant to teens.

As you can see from the following charts, stacking is not only helpful when building your individual portrait; it's also helpful when you're unpacking relationships and situations. When comparing people's stacked charts, it's easy to see where potential conflicts will emerge. Greg and Alejandro differ on many affiliations and values, and they frequently fall on opposite sides of the zone continuum. In part 3 we'll talk much more about how to unpack your relationships and interactions to understand the dynamics at play.

ALEJANDRO
AFFILIATION: AGE

Temperature	Hot / Age	Warm	Cold
Circle of Inclusion	Closed / Age	Selective	Open
Commitment	Activist / Age	Engaged	Passive
Strategy	Transform	Reform / Age	Conform
Power	High	Medium	Low / Age

ALEJANDRO
AFFILIATIONS: RACE AND AGE

Temperature	Hot / Race / Age	Warm	Cold
Circle of Inclusion	Closed / Race / Age	Selective	Open
Commitment	Activist / Race / Age	Engaged	Passive
Strategy	Transform / Race	Reform / Age	Conform
Power	High	Medium	Low / Race / Age

GREG
AFFILIATIONS: RACE AND AGE

Temperature	Hot	Warm	Cold
			Race
			Age
Circle of Inclusion	Closed	Selective	Open
	Race		
	Age		
Commitment	Activist	Engaged	Passive
			Race
			Age
Strategy	Transform	Reform	Conform
			Race
			Age
Power	High	Medium	Low
	Age		Race

Exercise: Building a Full Portrait

Now you can create an Identity Zone portrait by adding additional affiliations and values. Go back and select two or three more affiliations and values rated "A." Use the chart below as a model to build a fuller portrait of your identity.

Temperature	Hot	Warm	Cold
Circle of Inclusion	Closed	Selective	Open
Commitment	Activist	Engaged	Passive
Strategy	Transform	Reform	Conform
Power	High	Medium	Low

Full Portrait Implications

As you build your full portrait, you may start seeing certain patterns emerge across multiple affiliations and values. We've already talked about heat waves and cold fronts. But there are implications to tendencies in all the zones. Here are some things to keep in mind if you discover you're a hot personality or cold, a closed personality or open, an activist personality or passive, and so forth. I've tried to give one-liners to keep in mind for each of these tendencies. Of course, if you are a middle-of-the-zoner (warm, selective, engaged, etc.), you should keep *both* pieces of advice in mind, because you're likely to need them both at times.

> **Temperature: Hot.** Take a deep breath. If you are hot on several affiliations, you may be a hot personality. It's important to manage your emotional reactions without pushing others away. Being clear about the affiliation that actually causes you trouble at any specific time could be a challenge for you (one hot affiliation could "bleed over" to another). You have to take a deep breath and sort out the aspects of your identity that are threatened. Key ideas to ponder: overreacting, blaming, victimization, taking some personal responsibility, and patience with others.
>
> **Temperature: Cold.** Tune in. If you tend toward the cold end of the temperature continuum, then you may be out of touch with your actions or the dynamics that play out around you. Cold-front personalities may be absent during key moments where empathy, sensitivity, or conflict management skills are necessary. Things that aren't important to you may be very important to others, and you may have to tune in, learn more, and build your confidence in interacting with those who are hot. Key ideas to ponder: empathy, learning more about other perspectives, stretching to establish relationships with others who are outside of your of Circle of Inclusion.
>
> **Circle: Closed.** Search for commonalties. If you tend toward being closed, the challenge is to learn more about other perspectives that inhabit your day-to-day world. You have to know the basics about people in order to interact and not get tripped up. If you rely on information from limited sources, you will be woefully

unprepared to interact in a broader world and environment. Be careful not to harshly judge the experiences of those outside of your Circle of Inclusion Zone; try to look for commonality in other areas or affiliations. Community building is the issue here. Key ideas to ponder: multiple perspectives, innovative ideas, new ways of looking at things, new energy, potential support from others, and empathy.

Circle: Open. Be realistic. If you tend to be more open, try not to underestimate the comfort and security that some people require in order to function. It's easy to call others limited and narrow minded, but a closed or selective circle can help strengthen ties within groups that need empowerment. You may be too optimistic about what people are capable of at any given point in terms of tolerance and comfort with others. Forcing people to be open (without structure, supervision, and possibly education) is not always wise, especially in the United States, where we must be mindful of laws protecting people based on certain affiliations. Remember, just because you're open on an affiliation or value does not mean that everyone is or wants to be. Key ideas to ponder: naïveté, understanding, realism, and structure.

Commitment: Activist. Find pathways to balance. As an activist, you must make sure that you do not *become* your cause. Too much of a good thing is bad—even if the good thing is a worthy cause. If you become myopic and one-sided, you may act like a hammer for your cause and view everything (and everyone) as a nail. You will limit yourself to being only around people who share your fervor. You should not demonize those on the other side, keeping yourself in a constant state of war. If you can find joy through aspects of your other affiliations, that is the pathway to balance. Key ideas to ponder: balance, compromise, broader perspective, and backing off.

Commitment: Passive. Step up. As someone who is more disengaged, you don't have to care, but you may have to support people and issues that don't seem to affect you directly. Because we live and work with other people in a social and economic community, it stands to reason that their challenges eventually have an impact on your life. If fear holds you back, then self-empowerment is the issue. Where can you get support? Can you take baby steps toward improvement? Remember: your silence and lack of involvement is usually a subtle vote for one side or the other. Key ideas to ponder: assertiveness, stretching, support for others, investment, interdependence, and responsibility.

Strategy: Transformational. Explore Options. The challenges here are many: don't let rage lead you into violent conflict with the entire system when other options still exist. "Violence" can include economic, emotional, and spiritual aggression as well as physical acts. It's hard to make clean judgments about actions at the extreme left of the Strategy zone if you believe great events (revolution, the end of oppression, liberation) may be dependent on such action. Key ideas to ponder: clear vision, shared vision, patience, and building consensus.

Strategy: Conformist. Seek insight and understanding. If you chart more toward the conformist area within the zone, you may protect the old way of doing things as long as those who advocate change are left with limited options. If you invest in—and are served well by—existing systems and values, it may be more difficult to engage in discussions with those who have been locked out or treated unjustly without seeming defensive. When conflict erupts, your ability to observe and understand how the status quo negatively affects others will prove to be important. Key ideas to ponder: shared vision, multiple stakeholders, equal justice, responsiveness, and adaptability.

Power: High. Avoid arrogance. When you have the power, it's easy to slip into arrogance and insensitivity. When it feels like you can shape the environment and your world to fit your preferences and desires, you may forget that no one deserves to hold all the cards. If you belong to an affiliation group that possesses significant societal power, those outside that affiliation will think you are even more powerful than you are. You may see yourself as disengaged, not a contributor to intolerance, but they will see you as a beneficiary of injustice. Acknowledging this dynamic is an important step for you. Ideas to ponder: humility, compassion, justice, mercy, caring, and service to community.

Power: Low. Claim control. If you fall more toward the low power part of the zone, take small steps to claim more control over your environment and conditions. Be sure that you are not repressing anger and hostility, which has negative consequences on your well-being. Finding a positive outlet in a community with those who share your frustrations can be healing. Ideas to ponder: support, courage, inner strength, joining, community, using the resources within the system, and positive outlets to channel frustrations.

10

Your Identity Cycle

Why do we prioritize one affiliation over another? How do we get our zots? Why do we land where we do on the identity zone continuums? Our sensitivities and preferences evolve over time, influenced by a variety of factors and experiences. Now that you've charted some of your Identity Zones, you can deepen your understanding of yourself and the framework by thinking about

- How your life experiences have shaped your identity
- How your identity has *shifted* over time

When I was a child, being teased about my disability had a deep impact on me. I internalized the hurt and fear. I decided the best way to deal with the pain of being disabled was to hide it as best as I could. And it worked! I started living my life in a way that shielded me from prejudice and pity. Unlike my race, which was plain to see, my disability could be masked. I downplayed its significance for years, even to myself. Then

87

my identity began to shift. New experiences led to a new identity cycle, more relevant to this stage of my life journey.

It's worth keeping in mind that famous quote by George Santayana, "Those who cannot remember the past are condemned to repeat it." Our capacity to change as we age is immense. But sometimes we get "locked in" to negative patterns. Certain zots trigger a deep well of anger or pain that prevents us from connecting to others. Usually this is because of something that happened in the past—a hurtful event, an influential person, the social mores of a bygone era. Reflecting on your personal history, mining it for flashes of revelation, can help you evolve as a human being. Our identities are profoundly affected by the past. But they are not set in stone. They are in perpetual motion. This framework can give you the freedom to focus on a better future—one that is more fulfilling because it sustains more productive, meaningful relationships.

Laurie and Mark: The Finger Sandwiches

Sometimes in life we have an opportunity to gain insight into how our life experiences have contributed to our Identity Zones. I remember one such occasion vividly: October 30, 1995. The occasion was the third birthday celebration of my son. And I was witnessing something unbelievable: my wife Laurie coming unhinged because she'd spent two hours preparing *finger sandwiches* as a birthday "snack" for fifteen three-year-olds. These finger sandwiches were labors of love—cucumber, peanut butter and jelly, and, I swear to this day, some kind of pâté. She'd hand-cut them into stars, moons, and animal shapes. And the children had wasted no time in destroying all of her hard work, pulling the sandwiches apart, licking the insides out, smashing them into wads of gooey paste.

I could only shake my head in disbelief at what I was witnessing. And I have to admit: a part of me was laughing inside as Laurie stood horrified, watching her culinary triumph being dismembered. When she caught me mocking her, she shot me the glare that every spouse knows, which said, in no uncertain terms, "Okay, if you're so smart, next time *you* can do it!"

Laurie had, in my opinion, gone way overboard. Truthfully, I was embarrassed. No other birthday party for anyone under the age of twenty-one was so meticulously planned. Based on my three years of experience, every other child's birthday party had plastic forks, paper plates, a cake from the local store, and a paper tablecloth you used to gather up the garbage and then throw it away. I tried to make light of our over-the-top party with the other parents, so they were clear that this was "all Laurie." But they were busy using our silver and china to dig into the adult spread of platters of vegetables, cheese and crackers, sandwich wraps, and sparkling wine.

"Great party," said one of the other parents as they left. "You guys sure know how to throw a birthday bash!" said another. "It wasn't me," I said chagrined. "It was all her!" I heard the comments as dripping with sarcasm. Laurie heard them as genuine compliments. After everyone left, we quickly dissolved into our usual patterned disagreement about how much of what she does at parties is unnecessary. And how it's showy. She insists that it is a skill to entertain effortlessly. To me, "effortless entertaining" is an absurd way to describe her idea of a party. Typically, this disagreement spills out into a conflict about a half dozen other issues, from season tickets to theater or dance, to private school for the kids, to where and how we take vacations.

Identity Cycle Factors

The birthday party triggered zots for both Laurie and me. The zots can be predicted by differences within our respective Identity Zone charts. But when and where did these differences arise? In order to describe the origins of a predictable, repetitive pattern of conflict with my wife, I'm going to introduce some key factors that influence how our Identity Zones are formed, and then describe our two very different life paths and experiences.

1. **Time (Generational Context)**
   We're all products of our time. That's why marketers and the media love to give us names like "baby boomers" and "generation Xers." When we were born influences us because it matches

up with a certain social context. What was it like being an adolescent girl during the 70s, when the news was full of bra burning and women's lib? How is that different from being an adolescent girl when the secretary of state and the CEO of IBM are both women? When you were born, you stepped onto a stage that was already set, full of plots in midact. Your era—your century, your decade, your generation—will influence you consciously and unconsciously throughout your life.

2. **Place (Geographical Context)**
   Where you were born can be as important as *when* you born. Did you grow up in a rural, suburban, or urban setting? What was the socioeconomic structure, the class structure, the political climate? What were the prevailing social norms? The demographic profile? Many of your affiliations are based in geography (e.g., nationality, ethnicity, regional affiliation).

3. **Society (Social/Institutional Context)**
   What were the social norms, expectations, and values that influenced you most profoundly in childhood? These are functions of time and place, of course. They may be absorbed through your family, neighbors, and friends as well as major societal and civil institutions such as businesses, schools, the justice system, the political system, the media.

4. **Family Background**
   From our earliest days we're guided by our parents, our siblings, and the relatives who played an integral role in our childhoods. Our familes provide us with early lessons that help us understand how to cope with some of our innate affiliations—the challenges we face and the opportunities available to us. In childhood, we receive our first set of values, expectations, do's and don'ts, and survival and success strategies.

5. **Physical/Cultural Package (Innate Affiliations).**
   We're born with certain affiliations such as race, gender, nationality, and class. Some we can change, others we can't.

6. **Perspective.**
   We synthesize all of the above from an early age. We interpret conflicting data, internalize our experiences, and then integrate them into our own unique perspective. While our very first

childhood experiences are powerful, so, too, are the following decades. We shift our perspective after life passages like the birth of children, the death of loved ones, personal victories and defeats, and global events like war or terrorism.

Laurie and Mark: The Origins of Conflict

Now back to the finger sandwiches. Why did Laurie and I have a blowout after my son's third birthday party? Unpacking the incident later, I came to realize that I was viewing the situation based on the perspective of my teenage years in Virginia Beach. Let's take a closer look at my background and Laurie's to identify some of the origins of our conflict.

I grew up in a community where I enjoyed the benefits of a middle-class life, and where some of my friends, black and white alike, did not. It's true that during the '70s I still suffered the impact of bias and discrimination based on my race, but I also had opportunities that others did not, because I had two working parents. Many of my friends' families were proudly "making do" on one military wage. I never felt disadvantaged growing up. In fact, I felt advantaged. I had no contact with anyone who could be considered upper class until I went to college.

One of the clear values I learned growing up was that you did not show off. Other values were equally simple and straightforward. Don't take more than you can eat. Conserve resources and be thrifty. Help others who are less fortunate. And don't put on airs.

I learned to work hard, but I also learned that it was a good thing to kick back and relax, and relaxing in my community did not mean throwing elaborate parties. Enjoying one another while we were together was more important than "social etiquette." I learned that public schools were just fine (both my parents were public school educators). Going to a play was a fun thing to do every once in awhile. And summer vacation for the most part meant visiting the relatives.

You can sum up my identity cycle factors and my response to Laurie as follows:

I grew up in Virginia Beach, Virginia, during the late '60s, during the Vietnam War. Virginia Beach was a very conservative blue-collar/middle-class environment. I was not exposed to upper-class norms—except through the television shows *Dallas* and *Dynasty*. I never met anyone from such a background until college. I was proud to be a middle-class African American and I willingly embraced the values that came out of my experience. What happened at the birthday party? Laurie violated a middle-class value and put on airs! She embarrassed me! And she was "wrong."

Of course, Laurie didn't think she was wrong. Let's look at her perspective. Laurie grew up outside of Pittsburgh, Pennsylvania, during the 1960s and 1970s. Laurie was an upper-class girl whose father was a C-level executive in a major corporation and whose grandfather was the founder of a Fortune 500 company. Laurie's childhood was one of country clubs, chauffeured limousines, staff in the home, ballet, season tickets to major sports events, summers away for enrichment purposes, and, of course, lots of entertaining. She learned that reputations could be enhanced or diminished based on a dinner party. In her world, parties were judged to be a success or failure. The self-esteem of women, in particular, was measured by their ability to "effortlessly entertain." Their husbands relied on them to be gracious and sophisticated, for the sake of their careers.

Today, Laurie no longer embraces many of the values associated with her childhood. But she did internalize some of the expectations. She learned to appreciate the art of creating a memorable occasion, and she still takes pride in putting the pieces of an entertainment puzzle together well: setting the mood, creating the menu, and selecting the music, flowers, and wine. Inviting a successful mix of people to attend a dinner requires good people skills, and an ability to smoothly match and contrast interests, personalities, and stories to ensure a good time is had by all. Here's how Laurie describes her point of view in her own words:

> I know sometimes I can go overboard, but Mark doesn't fully appreciate all the details or effort involved in these events. Nor does he appreciate the sense of real joy and satisfaction I receive in entertaining.

Who is right? Well, we both are, of course. And through constantly pushing each other's zot on this issue we have "learned to learn from each other." Together, we have begun the Identity Cycle all over. And while we may never totally find the middle ground and tension will always exist, here is where we currently are in the cycle:

Time and Place. We both recognize that we are not in late-1960s America anymore, but in the twenty-first century. We do not have the resources that her family did, but we have more resources than what I grew up with. We are constantly negotiating how to best use those resources and what is of true value versus perceived social value. This comes out in our current debate about public versus private schools for our children.

Society. Laurie knows that she does not have to entertain to impress my clients or work colleagues because she is "the woman" and "the wife." She is much freer to choose from many alternatives available to women today to create their life and identity based on more personal values. I have learned to enjoy and appreciate some of the little luxuries that are available to people from a broad socio-economic range. It was Laurie who practically dragged me into Starbucks, which at first really offended my middle-class sensibilities. But now I am addicted. I can allow myself to enjoy a cup of fancy coffee without seeming to be putting on airs, knowing that although Starbucks is not affordable for everyone, it is also not an establishment reserved solely for the wealthy elite.

Family. Our families of origin are much less central to our day-to-day lives. Our two boys are growing up in an entirely different environment than either of us did. A real and present challenge for us is to honor the best of what we believe to be true from our childhood experiences, while accepting the vastly different time, place, and society that must guide us today. How many presents should the boys get? What kind of schools should they attend? What kind of vacation should we go on? What hobbies should we allow them to participate in? I tend to think that middle-class values are "right." Laurie tends to think that we should use more of our resources to provide a worldly backdrop for our children, so they are prepared to live in an expansive world. We are always struggling to meet in the middle.

Physical/Cultural Package. Of course, this includes our affiliations, and by now you understand that we are very different on the affiliation of socioeconomic background. Most of our conflicts and issues play out through this affiliation and closely connected values like our attitudes toward work and leisure. Laurie grew up in a community where status was in large part drawn from the success of the working father. Most of the mothers stayed home, tending to the home and children. Families in her community enjoyed many of the perks affiliated with the father's job status, and among these were vacations involving travel worldwide to first-class resorts. Her family took many vacations a year and viewed that travel as a time of edification and exposure, as well as meaningful family time. My family took one "vacation" each year to Mississippi, by car in the summer, to visit my mother's kin at the family farm as part of family duty.

Perspective. Laurie and I are aware that we trigger each other's zots on socioeconomic status. Many of the dilemmas we've learned to manage, and some we still have to work through. But armed with the knowledge that we have these sensitivities, we can usually catch ourselves before we dissolve into nonproductive conflict. Through our marriage, my perspective has changed because I have been forced to broaden my definition of "appropriate" to include many of the enrichments that Laurie brings to our lifestyle. Left to my devices, I would not have had many enriching experiences. I've become somewhat less judgmental and am not as quick to make knee-jerk accusations that she is going overboard. Laurie says her perspective has changed also. She seems to be able to let go more often and really relax into the moment, just hanging out with people, absent the formalities. I can set the table correctly and she can eat off of a paper plate every once in a while when we have friends over. And Laurie has become accustomed to spending fall and winter Sunday afternoons in front of the television, watching football, eating barbecue, rather than going to the ballet.

Exercise: Your Identity Cycle

Choose one of your top affiliations and use the following chart to reflect on how each aspect of the Identity Cycle has evolved over the decades.

Which of the following do you think most shaped your perspective of your affiliation?

- Family
- Geography/locale (nation, state, region, city)
- Community where you grew up
- Societal norms, values and laws
- Profession
- Your physical package
- Other affiliations
- Community where you live now

11

Your Solidarity Factor

I n this book I've focused primarily on the affiliations and values you claim as your own—your own race, your own gender, and so forth. I've included this chapter on the solidarity factor because I think we must acknowledge that a shared sense of sensitivity and solidarity with others can become an essential part of our identities—one that evolves out of a unique combination of affiliations, values, and life experiences.

Sometimes our zots can be triggered through affiliations and values that aren't our own. You can be extremely sensitive to race-related issues even though you're white, or extremely sensitive to age discrimination in the workplace even though you're a thirtysomething professional. In considering the solidarity factor, the question is whether you feel such a strong connection with a particular affiliation or value that you've come to own it as part of your identity. In some cases, this happens because we place a high value on fairness, justice, equality, or religion/spirituality. In other cases, this sense of solidarity grows out of a life experience that dramatically shaped your perspective.

Let me tell you about my friend Jean, who gave me unexpected support and encouragement when I went public with my disability. She came to me, shocked and sympathetic, after I made my announcement to my colleagues. Jean's aunt had a significant disability that left her wheelchair-bound from the time she was a little girl. Jean knew firsthand how her mother's life was altered because she had to assume greater responsibility for her sister while her parents worked. Her family lived in an era where there was little more than pity or disregard for "crippled" people.

Jean personally intervened on my behalf when the travel schedule would have had an impact on my health. Although not disabled personally, her family experience produced strong values on service and sensitivity to the disabled. If we chart Jean on her solidarity to disability, her temperature would be warm.

I know there are lots of Jeans out there—on many different issues. You can't make assumptions about zot reactions, even when dealing exclusively with people who are "just like you," because someone may feel real solidarity with those in other groups. You don't know everyone's history and you cannot ignore background information. Conflicts may arise when you make an insensitive remark, triggering someone's zot. Here are some examples of how affiliations and solidarity play out in people's lives:

- **Race.** Think about biracial or multiratial individuals, biracial couples, cross-racial adoptions.
- **Sexual Orientation.** Think about gay and lesbian parents, children, friends.
- **Nationality.** Think about second- and third-generation immigrants, cross-cultural marriages, families "back home" in another country.

Mel: A Story about Solidarity

Mel, fifty-two, is a thirteenth-generation, European American male, and former C-level executive at a half dozen Fortune 500 companies. He's been married for twenty-six years to his college sweetheart, Terri. They have a nine-year-old son. Well traveled and geographically astute, Mel has called both Maui and Washington, DC, home.

So, what can you say about Mel? Well, you might presume that he is an affluent, conservative Republican, married to a strong career woman who deferred motherhood until late in life. He probably comes from—and must live in—a never-ending world of privilege. Being politically and socially correct, Mel may tolerate diversity—but he does not embrace it.

These assumptions are all wrong. He grew up in rural Oregon, attended public schools, always held summer jobs, and worked his way through college. His diverse family is a palette of colors, ethnicities, and orientations. He and Terri had no grand designs to delay parenting; their son was both a surprise and a blessing. Mel made and lost millions in the wake of 9/11, the victim of bad luck and occasionally reckless optimism.

Mel's life experiences have helped him develop solidarity with people and groups whose affiliations he doesn't share. He consciously identifies himself more by values than affiliations—by spirituality, self-reliance, service, social responsibility, and world peace. Highly independent, he values the authenticity of personal experience and believes each of us needs to look inside in order to make our way to our envisioned destinies. Mel is distrustful of powerful institutions: churches, governments, and corporations. His life circumstances and perspectives have changed over time, but his values have not.

To truly know Mel, you have to know that the "solidarity factor" plays an important role in his sense of self, and that he has hidden zots based on his connection to affiliations you would never guess played a role in his life.

Solidarity Implications

We prioritize other people's affiliations and values, just as we do our own. Life experiences, life circumstances, and personal interest will lead us to embrace one cause over another, even if we have strong values on social justice, equality, or fairness for all. If you think of yourself as one who feels solidarity with people who are underrepresented or oppressed by society, beware of your "hidden" insensitivities—your blind spots to people who may need and/or deserve your empathy and understanding.

If you don't tend to feel solidarity with others, perhaps you've never experienced intolerance. Consider that at some point in your life, you or your loved ones may shift identities and suddenly learn what it feels like to feel unsupported, disrespected, or overlooked.

If you are a supervisor, teacher, or leader, you may be expected to reflect solidarity with certain affiliations and values, regardless of your personal feelings. Remember Greg? He was expected to participate in his company's mentoring program—despite his personal misgivings about the program. His company's management was largely white, but they were still hot and committed on race, and Greg had to adapt to his company's position.

Exercise: Solidarity Factor

Review the full list of affiliations/values and mark an "X" beside any that you feel solidarity with. Make sure to select any that you would lend some of your capital to, for any of the following reasons:

- They tap into your values of fairness and social justice and equality.
- You have a personal experience that heightens your sensitivity.
- You are responsible for the conduct of yourself, your team, or your organization when it comes to standards of sensitivity.

Next, think about any experiences you've had in which someone who didn't share your affiliations/values offered you support and encouragement. You can chart solidarity using the Temperature Zone, as I did below with Jean.

JEAN
ZONE: TEMPERATURE
AFFILIATION: PHYSICAL ABILITY

Temperature	Hot	Warm	Cold

Part 3

READING RELATIONSHIPS

Honest differences are often a healthy sign of progress.

—Mahatma Gandhi

Now that you've done the work of examining yourself, it's time to move forward into a new realm: using what you've learned in the previous chapters to begin improving your relationships. We'll cover many topics as we move forward, but throughout we'll be focusing on an essential skill: using Identity Zones to "read" and understand other people.

Putting this framework into practice will encourage you to put more emphasis on the relationships in your life. But before using the Identity Zone framework to understand relationships, you should take some time to reflect on your goals. Your goals may very well change during the process, but it is helpful to define a few objectives at the start. This will help you decide which information is needed and what actions you should take. While examining a relationship, try to periodically reconnect with your goals. Ask yourself: "Did I analyze the situation correctly? Am I achieving my goal? Has my goal changed?"

Here are some examples of goals:

To know/understand yourself better. You may simply want to build on what you learned in the first part of this book, identifying key affiliations, values, and Identity Zones through your interaction with others. If so, then you should use the framework primarily as a self-awareness tool.

To know/understand situations better by understanding the dynamics within your relationships. Perhaps you want to deepen your understanding of certain individuals by reading their affiliations, values, and Identity Zones. This goal implies that you will use the framework as an analytical tool.

To improve/deepen your relationships. Understanding the dynamic interplay or affiliations, values, and Identity Zones within a relationship can be a pathway to meaningful interaction and deeper levels of connection. This goal focuses on using the framework as a self-awareness, analytical, and strategic behavioral tool.

To better manage your zone-based conflicts. In the coming chapters, we will discuss how to diagnose zone-based conflicts. You will learn how to assess the potential consequences (risks and rewards) of such conflicts and change your behavior to minimize those risks (lawsuits, violence, and ineffective workplace dynamics). If this is your goal, the framework will be used as an analytical and strategic behavioral tool.

To mediate/resolve zone-based conflicts between family members, employees, customers, clients, or others. If you are a third party attempting to resolve a zone-based conflict, you can use the framework to guide individuals or groups toward operational strengths—not weaknesses. This goal focuses on using the framework as an analytical and strategic behavioral tool.

12

Reading the Nature of the Relationship

Throughout this book I've used real-life stories to help you understand the Identity Zones framework. I've written about my family, friends, colleagues, and clients—individuals from my social and community networks. I come into contact with people from all walks of life, so I have a rich pool of material to draw from representing the richness of today's multiworld. But my daily interactions are also multiple because they feature multiple contexts and multiple settings. Here are some of the key concepts you need to consider when thinking about the nature of your relationships and how to employ the Identity Zones framework:

- The *domain* you're operating in
- Your *level of investment*
- The *power dynamics* at play
- Whether you've encountered a *deal breaker*

Domains

All day long, as I hop from one relationship to another, I juggle different rules of interaction. I adjust my behavior to fit the norms, expectations, and laws of different contexts. These interactions take place in what I call *domains*:

- My family domain
- My professional domain
- My social domain
- My community or societal domain

Let's take a look at how domains affect my day. Working from home, I can spend the morning with my wife and kids (family domain), kiss them good-bye, and then drive down to my local coffee shop. There I spend a few minutes chatting with an employee named Gladys (community domain). Back home, I start working, which means talking on the phone or meeting in person with all kinds of people (professional domain). At lunchtime, sometimes I go out by myself to grab a sandwich (community domain), or I go to lunch with colleagues (professional and community domains). In the evening, we have family time (family domain).

Sometimes we have friends over for dinner (family and social domains), sometimes we go out to dinner or a movie (family and community domains), and sometimes we go out with friends (family, friends, and community domains). Occasionally, my wife and I meet one of my work colleagues for dinner (family, professional, and social domains) or at a function such as a fund-raiser (family, professional, social, and community domains).

As I move from domain to domain, the rules of interaction change. In my family domain, for example, I must work on responding sensitively, compassionately, and thoughtfully to my loved ones. But there's a built-in expectation in my family domain that we will sometimes disagree, that we'll push each other's zots from time to time. The emotional risks of confrontation here also carry substantial emotional rewards.

In my marriage, socioeconomic status is a source of zone-based conflict. Working through these differences isn't easy, and we often struggle to make joint decisions about our family life. Laurie and I have had more than one blowout on this issue. We've had heart-wrenching, soul-searching discussions. Is this emotionally risky? Yes, but we want to nurture healthy intimacy, a profound connection, and a deep level of understanding. Is it socially risky? Perhaps this is so, especially if our confrontation spills out into social or professional domains. Is it legally risky? Not unless the confrontation leads to divorce or violence.

By comparison, think about my relationship with Gladys, the coffee shop employee. Our relationship takes place in the community/societal domain. We usually chat for a few moments while she's preparing my coffee, and it's possible that one of us could stumble into a zot during one of these conversations. Once a zot is touched, the dynamic may change completely: We may do nothing, express mild annoyance, or blow up in anger.

Gladys's professional domain would govern her actions. The emotional and social risks are few for Gladys—but the professional risks are many, because her performance is partly measured in terms of customer satisfaction. My actions would be governed primarily by the expectations, norms, and rules of my community/society domain. If I rant and rave, I take no real professional or emotional risks: my job will not be threatened, nor will a profound connection be on the line. The legal risks are few, too, unless I become abusive or threatening. Socially, however, I am violating behavioral norms in a coffee shop full of strangers.

Level of Investment

Deciding how to respond to Gladys, as in all relationships, can be assessed in terms of investment. How invested am I in the relationship with Gladys? What do I risk by confronting her in this way? We can measure our investment in four ways, all tied to the very nature of the relationship:

- Transactional
- Casual/Collegial
- Friendship
- Intimate

Levels of investment must be considered together with domains to be meaningful. Below you can see my chart of my relationship with Gladys, which shows my perspective: both my level of investment and the domain where the relationship takes place.

MARK
RELATIONSHIP: GLADYS
CONTEXT: COFFEE SHOP

	Family	Social	Work	Community/ Social
Transactional				
Casual/Collegial				
Friendship				
Intimate				

Gladys's chart would be different, of course, since the relationship takes place in her work domain; only she could say for sure what her level of investment is. Let's walk through the various levels of investment and look at some additional examples of how they play out in different domains.

Transactional. When you're invested at the transactional level, you are only interested in results. If I only cared about good coffee, my relationship with Gladys would be purely transactional. Your community/society domain is full of transactional relationships with salespeople, bank tellers, flight attendants, and so on, but you can have a transactional relationship in any domain. Think of your co-workers, acquaintances, and even distant relatives. My friend Pam describes her relationship with her mother-in-law as purely transactional. They regularly trigger each other's zots because they share few commonalities across values and affiliations. The tension is always high when they interact, but (for the sake of her husband and son) Pam dutifully invites her mother-in-law to family gatherings, exchanges gifts and phone calls with her, and spends a week with her every year at the family beach house in South Carolina. Pam's level of investment is so low that when she thinks her mother-in-law is being insensitive or uncaring, she shuts her mouth, counts to ten, and leaves the room. She refuses to expend any energy on a relationship that seems to be going nowhere.

PAM
RELATIONSHIP: MOTHER-IN-LAW
CONTEXT: FAMILY GET-TOGETHERS

	Family	Social	Work	Community/ Social
Transactional				
Casual/Collegial				
Friendship				
Intimate				

Casual/Collegial. Relationships that begin as transactional often rise to the level of casual/collegial. This certainly happened in my relationship with Gladys. Because we converse every day for a few minutes, we've gradually established a bond. We've shared bits and pieces of personal information, so we have a limited understanding of each other's priorities and zones. She asks about my children; I ask about her college classes and homework. I enjoy the relationship, but I think it would be misleading to call her a friend just yet. Casual/collegial relationships tend to be extremely prevalent whenever group dynamics are at play—in workplaces, schools, neighborhoods, and community organizations.

Friendship. Friends invest in each other. The better the friendship, the more risks and rewards are available. In a true friendship, one not stuck in the transactional and casual/collegial phase, you seek out companionship, understanding, and mutual respect. This brings to mind my friend Barry, whom you first met in part 1 (the college roommate story). Barry and I have been through many phases of life together: college, career, marriage, parenting, and the deaths of loved ones. We've had a few serious disagreements over the years because of differences in the circle of inclusion zone. Zone-based conflicts often show us the difference between casual and true friendships: if we're not invested, one misunderstanding or confrontation may be enough to make us drop the relationship (severing the connection or moving it down to the transactional level). By working through the conflict, we may decide to invest more in the relationship and become better friends.

MARK
RELATIONSHIP: BARRY
CONTEXT: SOCIAL ENGAGEMENTS

	Family	Social	Work	Community/ Social
Transactional				
Casual/Collegial				
Friendship				
Intimate				

Intimate. With deep investment comes deep vulnerability. When we extend deep trust to another person, we want to be treasured, honored, and loved for both our strengths and our weaknesses. Let's look at my friends Emmit and Susan. They've been married for more than thirty years. They also co-own a small consulting business, so they end up spending 90 percent of their time together—working on projects, interacting with clients, and (in-between) sustaining a healthy marriage. They have to navigate zone-related tensions and guard against conflicts spilling over from the work domain to the intimate domain. On those occasions when their clients expect that Emmit is in charge because he is the man, which triggers Susan's zot on gender, they have to make sure that later that evening at home, the anger stays in the work domain. Impassioned, meaningful dialogue in one domain can lead to devastating consequences in another. Thus, it is highly difficult and highly rewarding to maintain cross-domain relationships with your intimates, whether they're spouses, relatives, or close friends.

EMMIT AND SUSAN
CONTEXT: HOME AND WORK

	Family	Social	Work	Community/ Social
Transactional				
Casual/Collegial				
Friendship				
Intimate				

Weighing Risks and Rewards

As we shift from domain to domain, we constantly shift gears according to our level of investment. Most of the time we do this unconsciously, fluidly, making choices about our behavior just because it "just feels right." But sometimes we need to be more conscious of our behavior. If your relationship falls into one of the categories below, consider the requisite actions.

Relationships in Zone-Based Conflict. If I notice red flags (which we'll discuss in more detail later) or an impending blowout, it's time to step back and ask myself about risks and rewards. These risks and rewards are based on the rules of the domain and my level of investment. Am I willing to get myself or someone else fired? Is it worth the energy? Do I care enough to move this relationship to the next level? Who will suffer if this relationship dies—me, my family, my company, and my community?

Relationships in the Professional Domain. You may be so invested in a professional relationship that you become friends, or perhaps even intimates. But don't assume that your friendship or intimacy, however genuine, moves this relationship into the social domain. When you step outside the professional environment to share a meal at lunchtime, the rules governing your behavior may still be influenced by professional norms and expectations—not social ones.

Relationships Impacted by a Nonneutral Power Dynamic. Power dynamics are part of every relationship: you may have more, less, or the same power as the other person, and each case creates a different dynamic between you. You should always take the time to consider how the power dynamic affects the nature of relationships, especially when one person wields significantly more power than the other. This category is worth investigating further.

Power Dynamics

In part 2, we talked about perceived power as one of the five Identity Zones. To refresh your memory, I divided perceived power into three subcategories:

- **Personal Power:** charisma, talent, intellect, self-confidence, determination, and persuasiveness
- **Situational/Hierarchal Power:** organizational rank or title, money, knowledge, resources, status, majority rule
- **Societal Power:** societal norms, ethics, laws

We created a chart based on your own perceived power, taking these three factors into account. Now, as we're looking at the nature of relationships, I'd like you to think about power again, but in another way. In some relationships, the distribution of situational power fundamentally changes things, creating new norms, expectations, and rules within the domain.

Consider an extreme example: your "relationship" with a king, dictator, or military ruler. This king commands all the resources of society and can, on a whim, have you detained or imprisoned. In this kind of relationship, what does it mean to be friends? Can you ever relax and let down your guard, trusting that your grievances will be heard and your feelings cherished?

Many relationships feature nonneutral power dynamics. Regardless of domain, these relationships are governed by unique sets of norms, expectations, and rules. In each of the relationships listed below, think about how the nonneutral power dynamic works.

- Boss–Subordinate
- Doctor–Patient

- Teacher–Student
- Parent–Child
- Employee–Customer
- Wife–Husband (within some cultures)
- First World Countries–Third World Countries
- Citizen–Law Enforcement Official

At one point in my career, I learned one of the golden rules about power dynamics: *he rules who has the gold!* I was involved with a client project that was near and dear to my heart. I poured a lot of my creative energy into the project and knew that the work would lead to real organizational transformation. But, despite the accepted goals of the project, the company didn't really want transformation. Through various committees, my clients continued to offer obstruction and unfocused feedback. They requested alterations that fundamentally altered the original intent of the work.

Usually willing to accommodate client needs, I also have a strong value on integrity. In this instance my zots on integrity were being triggered. I felt I was being forced to choose: client responsiveness versus the integrity of the work and the values of my profession. Everyone picked up on the red flags as our interactions became more difficult and contentious, so we agreed to meet and repair our communication issues.

I thought we were colleagues in a professional environment, and that we would collaboratively address our differences on the intent of the project. Within a few moments, however, a senior VP entered the room and told me that he had heard complaints about me. I was not accommodating client needs, he said, and if this continued the project would be terminated and I would be replaced. "Any questions?" he asked. "Nope," I said. I understood then that the VP considered the relationship with me purely transactional. Furthermore, he had all the situational power, because he had control of the money. The power dynamic was not neutral, and my choice was simple: shape up or ship out.

Deal Breakers

In every relationship, there are commonalities and differences. By digging deeper, we can build, improve, and enrich relationships based on commonalities. But sometimes the process of digging uncovers a deal breaker. Deal breakers are affiliations or values that are high priority, red hot, or profoundly influenced by negative interactions within a specific zone—or, most likely, all three. A deal breaker puts a complete stop to all relationship building.

My wife, Laurie, ended a relationship based on a deal breaker. Laurie and I used to socialize regularly with another married couple: Trisha and Lars. Trisha is a delight; everyone loves her, wants to spend time with her, and feels enriched by a relationship with her. But Lars is different. Lars projects an attitude that many people find alienating. At his worst he acts as if he knows everything, is always right, and professes to be an accomplished expert in every possible field. He laughs at his own jokes, interrupts others, and is generally bombastic and argumentative. One night, when the four of us were out together, Lars infuriated us all. He started making derogatory comments about the poor state of the Washington, DC, public school system.

"How can any responsible person," he asked, "send their children to school in Washington, DC? Anyone who does so should lose their license as a parent." Laurie patiently explained that this was an unrealistic attitude. Most parents had no choice. Who would take care of all these kids, if these parents "lost their licenses?" Three of us laughed, but Lars did not.

Lars basically called my wife a bleeding-heart liberal and went on to blame all liberals for the current public education mess. Laurie was livid; she told Lars that he should have some children before expressing his views on parenting. The discussion eventually wound down, but the damage had already been done. The four of us did not get together again after that episode.

I encouraged Laurie to talk about her feelings, but the bottom line was that she did not want to invest in the relationship with Lars anymore. She could remain friends with Trisha, but she also knew that other people over the years had tried to reason with Lars to no avail. The combination of his personal style, his treatment of others, and his values and affiliations triggered Laurie's zots and became a deal breaker for the relationship. There was no turning back.

If you tend to be closed, you may use your affiliations and values as deal breakers. My friend Olivia—the one who went on a blind date—

ended that relationship because her date had radically different political ideas and affiliations. That was a deal breaker for her; no matter
how attractive or interesting the man was, there was no chance for a
relationship.

We shouldn't use deal breakers as a convenient excuse to bow out
of relationships. We shouldn't ignore others just because we are
uncomfortable dealing with them, and we shouldn't be afraid of
divisive issues. On the other hand, beware when you encounter the
following:

- Physical or verbal abuse
- Attacks or regular explosions
- Blaming others first
- Can't be wrong
- Distorting the truth; dishonesty
- The same speech over and over
- The same complaints over and over
- Grinding an ax
- Refusal to take any responsibility
- Mean spirited
- Overly judgmental

See chapter 20 for more about danger signs in conflicts.

Exercise 1: Domain/Investment Chart

Let's use the chart below to examine one of the relationships in your life.
Begin by selecting one of the domains on the top line. (Note: if more
than one domain applies, as it does for Emmit and Susan, then feel free
to make more than one choice.)

Now, select the level of investment that you have in your relationship
(listed on the left side of the chart). If more than one level applies, you
can make more than one choice. Many people in the modern workplace,
for example, are both collegial and friendly. One aspect of the relationship takes place at work and the other takes place in the social community arena.

DOMAIN VERSUS INVESTMENT

	Family	Social	Work	Community/ Social
Transactional				
Casual/Collegial				
Friendship				
Intimate				

Exercise 2: Power Dynamics

What is the power dynamic of your selected relationship? Does it fall into one of these categories?

- Neutral: neither of you has role power over the other.
- Your Power: you have the role power.
- Their Power: they have the role power.

Now do a risk-reward analysis. Think about your relationship, the affiliations/values that are in play, the domain that you are operating within, and the power dynamic. Use a pen or pencil to mark your place somewhere on the continuum below:

If you take the lead in shifting the dynamic of this relationship how would you assess the potential risk?

High Risk ———————————— Low Risk

If you take the risk to shift the dynamic of this relationship how do you assess the potential reward?

High Reward ———————————— Low reward

13

Deciding What's at Play

There is a famous Buddhist parable about the nature of observation. There are many different versions of the tale, but it goes something like this: a prince asks a group of blindfolded men to describe an exotic creature they've never seen—an elephant. He presents each man with a different part of the animal to touch—a tusk, a leg, an ear, a tail. None of the men gets a clear picture of the whole beast. One says an elephant is like its tusk, hard and smooth. Another says an elephant is like its tail, thin and hairy. And so on. In some versions of the story, the men argue heatedly and eventually come to blows over which is the "true" description of the elephant.

When you're using the Identity Zones framework, you're trying to see the whole elephant. This means you're trying to gain perspective, adjusting your telescope, accounting for your own blindfolds. You're also trying to decide what's at play. Which affiliations and values are having an impact on your relationships? Which Identity Zones are producing tensions? When a conflict or misunderstanding arises, what combination of factors is heating up the situation? Every meaningful human interaction creates a potentially volatile brew of affiliations, values, and Identity Zones.

If you're trying to diagnose a conflict, in short, you want *information*. The more the better. Some information will present itself in the moment, when temperatures heat up and/or zots get triggered. Other information may be stored in your memory. After the moment has passed, you may have to work to unpack the conflict and recall what you know. Sometimes, if you decide it's worth the risk, and your level of investment is significant, you may ask somebody to give you information about themselves—but, of course, this must be done delicately, as we'll discuss more in part 4, "Crossing the Zones."

In this part of the book I'll give you some tools you can use to gather more information—to diagnose conflict and to chart your relationships. We'll focus in depth on two stories about real-life conflicts. We'll discuss

- Reading the signs of zone-based conflict
- Charting relationships
- Deciding which affiliations and values are at play
- Using indicators (reading zones)
- Adjusting your telescope (checking your work)
- How group dynamics have an impact on conflict

Reading the Signs of Zone-based Conflict

With practice, you will get better at reading situations and relationship dynamics by using the Identity Zones framework. Perhaps this is one of your goals for reading this book: to learn to stop trouble before it starts, avoiding potential conflicts. A worthy goal! In the beginning, however, you're wise to remember that most of us learn about other people's zots by accident. We say or do something that acts as a trigger. Suddenly, we're in the midst of an uncomfortable moment, or even a blowout—a zone-based conflict with damaging consequences.

One of the ways you can diagnose what's happening in your relationships is to train yourself to read the signs of zone-based conflict. I call these signs red flags, as a reminder that they're potential signs of zone hotspots, or zots. When you're looking for red flags, you have to look both ways, at yourself and others, to see whether affiliations or values are creating tension. Do you feel hurt, angry, or misunderstood? Have you offended someone? Has your zot or someone else's zot been triggered? Are your zones out of sync with someone else's? Is there a relationship at risk? In a group or organizational setting, are people with certain affiliations and values excluded or treated insensitively? If you're not sure whether the roots of an argument can be traced to Identity Zones, it's time to start looking for red flags.

Gavin and Maria: The Party

Let me tell you a story about some married friends of mine who stand on opposite sides of the political spectrum. Gavin is a policeman, a Republican from Wyoming. Maria is a schoolteacher, a Democrat from California. They often socialize with a core group of Maria's friends, which includes some extremely liberal Democrats. At a party one evening, Gavin nearly blew his top. Let's let Gavin tell the story:

> I usually don't let Maria's friends get to me, but that night was different. They ranted and raved about a political leader who I happen to admire. They called him stupid and evil; they talked about his supporters with contempt. They all knew my politics, but they just didn't care. By the end of dinner I was furious. I took Maria aside and told her I wanted to leave. At home, I made it clear that I found that kind of situation unacceptable. I didn't want to come between Maria and her friends, but if she loved me, she should speak up more on my behalf. She should tell them what she really believes: Republicans aren't all stupid or evil, or she wouldn't have married one.

In the case of Gavin and Maria, a number of red flags were present before and during the dinner party:

- In the past, Gavin had made offhand comments about her friends being over the top, a little too much, too intense, and so on.
- During past social events, the group typically split into clusters based on political temperature, commitment, and strategy;

Gavin gravitated toward those who were in the middle of the political continuum.

- During the party, Gavin shut down. He withdrew from the conversation and stopped speaking up in defense of his beliefs.
- Gavin's only comments after he shut down came through his body language: shaking his head, crossing his arms protectively in front of his chest, glancing at Maria as if to say, I can't believe I'm being assaulted/disrespected in this way.

Maria may have missed the red flags during the party, but she paid attention to Gavin when he shared his perspective and his feelings. When someone confronts you, as Gavin confronted Maria, red flags can help you stand back and see his or her concerns as part of a zone-based conflict. Consider it an opportunity: if you engage in this moment with sensitivity and respect, you may avoid further conflict and perhaps open the door for a fruitful discussion. Maria apologized for not noticing her husband's pain and discomfort. She pledged to remind her friends not to demonize other political affiliations. She also encouraged Gavin to speak up when his views were the object of hostility or scorn. This is the important lesson: they avoided a major blowout with serious consequences (such as lingering anger, open hostility, resentment, or worse).

Common Red Flags

Red flags come in many shapes and sizes. I've tried to identity some common red flags, breaking them out according to signs displayed by an individual, signs within a relationship, and signs in groups/organizations.

When an individual is angry/hurt/disrespected, based on Identity Zones you may notice these red flags:

- Cold, distant, less friendly, withdrawn
- Doesn't voice opinions/share ideas
- Closed body language (rolling arms, crossed arms)
- Tone of voice (sarcasm, suspicion)
- Whispering, saying things under breath

- Argumentative (always challenging, never agreeing)
- Subtle cries for help (offhand comments, threats)
- Walking out
- Avoiding each other

In relationships where Identity Zones are causing problems you may notice these red flags:

- Petty conflicts
- Patterns of conflict/miscommunication
- Passive-aggressive behavior
- Flashes of unexplained/inappropriate hostility
- Mutual sense of confusion or frustration
- A sense that you're not really getting at the issues
- Feeling of dread/anticipation about interacting
- Avoiding interaction
- Sadness, disappointment, hurt feelings
- Use of sarcasm or jokes

In groups where Identity Zones are causing problems (in addition to the above) you may notice:

- Clusters or factions
- Exclusionary behavior
- Polarization
- Inability to reach consensus
- Sabotaging
- Loss of momentum and efficiency
- Lack of pride
- Unwillingness to take risks
- Unwillingness to go the extra mile

Ignoring red flags is nearly always risky. Even if you never experience a blowout, the feelings of hurt or anger may stay on a back burner, still causing damage. When left simmering, zone-based conflicts almost always produce unhealthy, unsatisfying, unproductive patterns in one-on-one relationships and groups.

Unpacking the Relationship

Once you've decided you're definitely dealing with a zone-based conflict, you can start unpacking it, trying to identity the affiliations and values at play. Eventually, if you decide your level of investment is high enough, you may wish to begin charting your relationship, stacking your charts together to get a better picture of "the whole elephant."

The process of charting the relationship has four parts. We've already done step one:

1. Charting your domain/investment and calculating risks and rewards (see chapter 12)

Now we'll move on to steps 2–4, which use many of the concepts we introduced in part 2, "Knowing Yourself":

2. Deciding which affiliations and values are at play
3. Using indicators to "read" the other's zones
4. Adjusting your telescope (checking your work)

Deciding Which Affiliations and Values Are at Play

It's probably human nature to look for one problem to hang our hats on. In relationships, especially ones with colleagues or casual acquaintances, it's tempting to assume that a single affiliation or value is the source of tension. We think, it's because I'm black and she's white, it's because I'm poor and he's rich, it's because I value creativity and all they care about is structure. But relationship problems don't arise in a vacuum. You can't conveniently deal with one affiliation or value at a time. If you behave like the men with the elephant, grabbing hold of a single part of a complex dynamic, you'll miss crucial information.

Let me tell you another story. This time, I'm going to describe a serious zone-based conflict—one that ends in a blowout with damaging consequences.

Ann and Robert: The Chicken Wing Incident

Several years ago, I was a part of a team that had an important meeting with a client in a small western town. I arrived the night before with six colleagues—four men and two women—all of us hungry and exhausted from the long flight. We asked the hotel clerk for a restaurant recommendation and were told that almost everything in town closed by 10 p.m. The clerk directed us to a restaurant called Hooters, "with a casual atmosphere and great chicken wings." He also mentioned (in terms I won't repeat here) that the restaurant was famous for its attractive, provocatively dressed waitresses.

Two of my colleagues immediately spoke up. Robert ignored the comment about the waitresses and focused on the chicken wings, which sounded good to him. Ann, on the other hand, said we should refuse to patronize any business that was sexist and exploited women. Robert laughed at Ann's concerns, and Ann grew more and more indignant. Other team members began to withdraw. One of our more junior team members said she would "just grab something to eat" and go to her room. We persuaded her to stay. There was no room service available at that hour. Where was she going to go? To the vending machines in the lobby?

Meanwhile, Robert and Ann kept going back and forth, Robert needling Ann, Ann passionately defending her perspective. Someone suggested a compromise: that we order the wings from the restaurant and then go pick them up. Ann would have none of that, insisting that we couldn't give our dollars to an oppressive organization. To support her point, she mentioned a recent article about the damaging impact that the chain had on women's self-esteem and the negative message that it sent to young girls about their sexuality.

Robert thought this analysis was heavy-handed. He accused Ann of taking this all too seriously, killing the team spirit and "forcing her political agenda" on the group. This was clearly going too far. But by the time the rest of us stepped in, sensing a potential blowout, Ann was already spiraling out of control. She was shaking with anger and couldn't let it go, even after Robert relented. We found another restaurant, but Ann continued to seethe. She thought the incident signaled larger problems within her working relationships. Later on, Ann told me that she didn't think she could work with Robert anymore. The Chicken Wing Incident nearly ended their professional association.

Ann and Robert: Deciding What's at Play

Let's start unpacking. The most obvious thing at play in this conflict was gender. Why? Robert and Ann were of opposite genders, and the argument was about gender insensitivity. Later, we'll talk more about where each fell within the zone continuums, and how we came up with their charts. For now, trust me when I say that Ann is hot on gender. She is deeply, personally, painfully sensitive about the way gender has affected her life and the lives of other women. But if you were to assume that nothing else but gender was at play, you'd miss the bigger picture. Look beyond gender to the value of social justice/equality, for example. This is one of Ann's core values. In addition to fighting against gender discrimination, she believes in fighting for justice and equality regardless of her personal stake in the issue. She is white but fights racial discrimination. She is middle class but fights poverty. The solidarity factor plays a big role in her life.

The tension ratcheted up when Ann started arguing with Robert and found her arguments on gender *and* social justice/equality falling on deaf ears. In her view Robert was hopelessly out of touch, unaware, insensitive, and uncaring about the injustices of the world.

Humor was also a pivotal value in this incident. Humor is a core value for Robert. With all of us tired and cranky, he mistakenly assumed he could diffuse tension by cracking jokes about chicken wings and scantily clad waitresses. This didn't go over well with Ann, of course, which triggered a zot in Robert. Why was she being so serious? Why couldn't she lighten up? Couldn't she see he was only joking? If you look at their charts on humor and social justice, you can see these two were destined to clash on these values as well.

ZONE: TEMPERATURE
VALUE: HUMOR

Temperature	Hot (ROBERT)	Warm	Cold (ANN)

ROBERT AND ANN
VALUE: SOCIAL JUSTICE

Temperature	Hot (ANN)	Warm	Cold (ROBERT)

Deciding What's at Play: Helpful Guidelines

Remember that your perspective is limited. When you're unpacking, you need to ask yourself whether you're overlooking the full range of affiliations, values, and Identity Zones that are affecting your relationships and interactions. If you've got that mystified feeling: what's wrong with her? Why isn't he listening? What is she talking about? You could be stuck so deeply in your own perspective that you're missing a piece of the puzzle.

Don't revert to preconceived notions.

They can be a trap when you're determining what's at play. Remember the story about the two men who clashed over a press release at work? Everyone thought it was a conflict about race. Sensing the tension, the senior VP—the one who painted a rosy picture on the release—bent over backward to try to prove that he wasn't prejudiced. He found ways to work his race-based activism, his support of mentoring and advocacy groups. Of course, his employee was baffled, because in his mind, race wasn't the issue at all. Honesty was the issue. The boss had violated one of his core values by stretching the truth in front of stakeholders, board members, and the media.

During the Chicken Wing Incident, Ann decided Robert was insensitive (cold) on gender. When Robert kept joking with Ann, she saw him growing colder, and colder, and colder. She saw his jokes purely as a sign of his indifference, his lack of caring, his insensitivity about gender issues. It didn't occur to her that he was joking because humor was one of his core values. There was another conflict at play (cold on humor vs. hot on humor) that she didn't recognize until much later, after the blowout's consequences had already played themselves out.

Remember commonalities.

When I introduced the married couple Gavin and Maria, I mentioned that they have different political affiliations. Based on the story I told, you might wonder: how do Gavin and Maria make their marriage work, when they have such different political beliefs and different friends? What I didn't mention are all the affiliations and values that they have in common. I didn't tell you that they're both patriotic Americans who love living in Washington, DC. I didn't tell you they're both Christians, both deeply committed to living life with honor and integrity. I didn't mention that they can be found together every morning at the gym, or running side by side along the Potomac River, because they're both dedicated to staying physically fit.

Neither Gavin nor Maria is truly hot on political affiliation. They each fall somewhere between warm and hot, not at the extreme end of the continuum. When pressed, neither of them places political affiliation in their list of high-priority affiliations and values. If you put aside the dinner party for a moment and dig deeply into their relationship, you can begin to glimpse the foundations of their marriage, which has been built on commonalities that help bridge their differences. Here's how their priority lists look stacked side by side:

GAVIN AND MARIA'S SHARED AFFILIATIONS AND VALUES

	Gavin	Maria
Affiliations	**Nationality**	**Nationality**
	Regional affiliation	Regional affiliation
	Religion	Religion
	Marital status	Marital status
	Military experience	Education
Values	**Love of country**	**Love of country**
	Integrity	Integrity
	Physical appearance/Fitness	Physical appearance/Fitness
	Fidelity/Loyalty	Friendship
	Self-reliance	Social justice/Equality

Note: Gavin and Maria's shared affiliations and values are shaded.

When our differences are obvious, it's easy to become consumed by them. In a context like Washington, DC, politics is everything, right? Wrong. A difference in political affiliation can be dwarfed by commonalities. Digging deeper lets us find commonalities. When an intimate relationship is in conflict or under stress, we need to dig down to the foundation of commonalities that brought us together in the first place. When red flags crop up in a casual or professional relationship, it's time to start digging deeper, looking for commonalities that can help you work through potential conflicts.

Look again at the lists of Gavin and Maria's priorities. These stacks of affiliations and values help us see the priorities they share in common. They show where they differ. But the lists only scratch the surface. What did you learn from drawing your portrait? There are infinite variations to your identity and to other people's identities as well. Put them together and the variations multiply. Consider the stacks upon stacks of affiliations/values, the shifting priorities, the degrees of differences within each zone: temperature, circle of inclusion, commitment, style, power. Consider some of the complex dilemmas and the interwoven affiliations/values Gavin and Maria faced during a single moment in their marriage, at a dinner party in Washington. Let me tell the story again from a "whole elephant" perspective.

Gavin is a policeman with a military background. He is drawn to the Republican Party because he believes it reflects more of his core values and affiliations, including love of country, support of the military/law enforcement, and a focus on self-reliance and Christian beliefs. Maria is a teacher. She is drawn to the Democratic Party, in part, because she believes it supports education and reflects her commitment to social justice/equality issues, as well as Christian ethics of charity and compassion. Neither of them is red hot on political affiliation, but there were many other values/affiliations in play at that dinner party, including:

Marital Status. At the time of the party, Gavin and Maria had been married less than a year. They were still trying to navigate new territory, and each was highly sensitive about trying to work through their differences.

Fidelity/Loyalty. Gavin felt blowing up at the party would be disloyal to Maria, hurting her by hurting her friends.

Friendship. Maria found it agonizing to choose between staying out of it or speaking up, because this felt like choosing between her friends and her husband.

Regional Affiliation. Gavin and Maria love living in the heart of Washington, where strong political opinions and lively debates are part of the local flavor. When the political became personal, each of them was forced to decide when to "draw the line."

Integrity. Gavin and Maria felt the push and pull of their own internal honor codes in this situation. Expressing their true beliefs, allowing others to express theirs, refusing to be "dragged down" to the level of name calling—the tension increased because they both wanted to do the "right" thing and expected the same from their spouse.

When two people are in conflict, it's as if they've stepped onto a stage. Ready, set, action! The curtain opens and we're in the middle of an exciting plot that moves along with the help of props, gestures, lines, supporting actors, and so forth. We forget all about what's going on behind the scenes, the makeup artists, the green room, the dusty old curtains, the invisible ropes that whisk things up and down. What's offstage might as well disappear. Except, of course, when what's offstage is the rest of our lives, the rest of the world, a vast universe of important people, things, and events.

Ann and Robert stepped onto a stage during the Chicken Wing Incident. With all the zots at play in the conflict—gender, social justice/equality, humor, et cetera—they didn't step back to catch their breath. And they didn't think about an extremely important thing that was hovering in the wings offstage: our presentation to the client the next day. Ann and Robert were key members of our team. The conflict was shining a spotlight on their differences, but we all knew they were capable of working well together, because they shared some common values, including professionalism, responsibility, and structure.

One way to reduce tension in a zone-based conflict is to move the spotlight away from what's at play to what's not at play, shifting the emphasis from differences to commonalities. When this works, it can change blowout mode to discussion mode, and you can handle the conflict with less damaging consequences.

Exercise: Deciding What's at Play

Below is a list of affiliations and values. These were also at play in the Chicken Wing Incident. Can you imagine why and how? Remember that this blowout started with an argument about patronizing a business Ann believed exploited women.

- Socioeconomic status
- Physical appearance
- Professional affiliation
- Education
- Self-reliance
- Belonging/fitting in
- Humor

Using Indicators (Reading Zones)

While there were multiple values and affiliations at play in the Chicken Wing Incident, I think we can still agree that gender was the primary source of the conflict—the place where it all began. So let's start there and dig deeper, further unpacking the conflict to look at where Robert and Ann fell on the zone continuums. We can do this by going back to the zone indicators we introduced in part 2. Zone indicators are a useful tool when you're reading other people's zones, either in the moment or after the fact—whenever you think you have enough information to begin to assess the other person's feelings/behaviors.

Here's what we know about Ann based on temperature indicators:

Political/Community Awareness. Ann characterized the women's jobs at the restaurant in political and economic terms.

Language Awareness. Ann became more indignant and upset at how Robert characterized the situation using words Ann considered offensive.

Humor Sensitivity. Ann did not laugh at Robert's jokes (and neither did anyone else, after a certain point). Robert loved to make others laugh and jokes were a big part of his personality. He even made jokes about men and would laugh at the foibles of his own gender.

Bonding/Solidarity. Ann felt a bond with the waitresses in the restaurant.

Deeply Held Convictions. Ann had very strong, serious opinions about the restaurant. Hers was not a spontaneous irrational reaction.

Media Awareness. Ann quoted an article that had been written about this restaurant chain and its controversial impact on women.

Robert wasn't thinking about affiliations or values when he lobbied to go to the restaurant. He focused on "the best chicken wings in town" and ignored everything else. If he had paid closer attention, he would have read Ann's unusually strong reactions based on the Temperature Zone Indicators and realized that she was hot on the affiliation of gender.

Once Ann knew that gender was the primary affiliation that was at play in her conflict with Robert, and that her zot had been triggered on this affiliation, she could have taken a step back, and assessed where Robert fell within the Temperature Zone, and figured out (as the rest of us did) that Robert was ice cold on gender and completely unaware of the impact of his behavior.

Let's take a look at how Ann and Robert chart together in the Temperature Zone of gender, which is at the center of their conflict:

ANN AND ROBERT
AFFILIATION: GENDER

Temperature	Hot (ANN)	Warm	Cold (ROBERT)
Circle of Inclusion	Closed	Selective	Open
Commitment	Activist	Engaged	Passive
Strategy	Transform	Reform	Conform
Power	High	Medium	Low

Now let's take a closer look at how Ann's strong feelings about gender play out across all five zones, as reflected in her behavior and lifestyle. We'll use indicators to assess her place on each zone continuum.

Ann on Gender: Circle of Inclusion Zone

Indicator: Where you live
Ann lives in a neighborhood equally populated with both men and women.

Indicator: Where you work
Ann works in an organization staffed by equal numbers of men and women; however, she spends her social time at work (lunches, etc.) primarily with female coworkers.

Indicator: Critical service providers
Ann actively seeks out women service providers such as doctors, legal professionals, and accountants.

Indicator: Membership in social organizations
Ann is an active member and played a leadership role in several women's organizations.

Indicator: Social life
Ann spends the majority of her social time with women; she has a very strong group of women friends who support each other in every aspect of their lives.

Indicator: Sources of information
Ann reads women's trade magazines, watches cable programs for women, and subscribes to Web sites for women.

Based on these indicators, I would place Ann somewhere in the middle of the Circle of Inclusion continuum, as indicated on her Gender Identity Zones chart.

ANN
AFFILIATION: GENDER

Temperature	Hot	Warm	Cold
Circle of Inclusion	Closed	Selective	Open
Commitment	Activist	Engaged	Passive
Strategy	Transform	Reform	Conform
Power	High	Medium	Low

Ann on Gender: Commitment Zone

Indicator: Speaking up
Not only did Ann speak up in the Chicken Wing incident, but she has always been very vocal on women's issues in general. Ann will always point out inequities in treatment between men and women, regardless of the environment.

Indicator: Joining/Bonding
Ann regularly speaks up on behalf of younger, less-senior women. She belongs to professional networking groups dedicated to empowering women in their careers.

Indicator: Donating/Volunteering
Ann has volunteered at shelters for victims of domestic violence, and she regularly donates money to women's causes. She brings some of these causes to her coworkers' attention, asking for their support.

Indicator: Advocacy/Spreading the word
Ann spreads the word about companies with a reputation for treating women unfairly. She also knows which companies are rated as best places to work for women. She makes a point of supporting companies that make products focusing on women's strength, confidence, and inner beauty, rather than their sex appeal.

Indicator: Voting/Political involvement
Ann has a litmus test for candidates; she wants to know exactly where they stand on several key issues that she thinks are vital to the well-being of women.

Based on these Commitment indicators, I would guess that Ann is an Activist, as indicated on her chart.

ANN
AFFILIATION: GENDER

Temperature	Hot	Warm	Cold
Circle of Inclusion	Closed	Selective	Open
Commitment	Activist	Engaged	Passive
Strategy	Transform	Reform	Conform
Power	High	Medium	Low

Ann on Gender: Strategy Zone

Indicator: Advocating a new vision
Ann believes the modern workplace is based on the cultural norms, styles and preferences of men, not women. She thinks it's time for a new, women-centric approach—a workplace that reflects the increasingly vital role played by women.

Indicator: Breakthrough or innovative concepts
Ann advocates redefining professional competency measurements to include more of the qualities she believes women bring to the table. Her idea is to encourage men to adapt and develop new skills, just as women have adapted and developed new skills in order to succeed professionally. She thinks this might prove beneficial to both genders.

Indicator: Degree of revolutionary thinking
Ann supports the existing system, but also advocates pushing it to be all that it can be.

Indicator: Investment in the existing system and norms
While Ann works for change, she also lives a relatively mainstream lifestyle, living and socializing with both men and women, and working within a professional system she sees as biased.

Indicator: Willingness to go to war or do battle
At least to the outside observer, Ann shows no evidence of a battle mentality, although she participates in peaceful protests and marches on occasion.

Indicator: Sense of urgency
Again, there is no evidence that Ann feels an overwhelming sense of urgency about gender issues.

Indicator: The end justifies the means
Ann does not use dramatic, aggressive, violent, all-or-nothing tactics to address her concerns about gender and women's issues.

Ann is not at the extreme left side of the strategy continuum; she isn't operating outside the law or using aggressive tactics. However, Ann is deeply committed to changing the way women are treated in society and the workplace, and she envisions a new approach to gender-based systems and norms. I would place her somewhere between Reformist and Transformational on the continuum.

ANN
ZONE 4: STRATEGY
AFFILIATION: GENDER

Temperature	Hot	Warm	Cold
Circle of Inclusion	Closed	Selective	Open
Commitment	Activist	Engaged	Passive
Strategy	Transform	Reform	Conform
Power	High	Medium	Low

Ann on Gender: Power Zone

Indicator: Personal power

In most public or professional situations, Ann is confident that when she speaks, people will listen, take her opinions seriously, and often follow her advice.

Indicator: Situational/Hierarchal Power

Ann is a senior consultant and is respected. She manages junior consultants, and she is part of the leadership team within her consulting firm.

Indicator: Societal Power

Ann thinks the society is still biased toward men, but she sees the norms slowly changing. That's why she was so forceful during the Chicken Wing Incident. She thought it was inappropriate, in this day and age, for a group of professionals to patronize such an establishment.

Based on the power indicators, Ann seems to have a relatively high degree of perceived power; she feels empowered to demand fair treatment and speak up about the legacy of sexism, especially in the workplace, and she expects her views to be respected and validated.

ANN
ZONE 5: POWER
AFFILIATION: GENDER

Temperature	Hot	Warm	Cold
Circle of Inclusion	Closed	Selective	Open
Commitment	Activist	Engaged	Passive
Strategy	Transform	Reform	Conform
Power	High	Medium	Low

We now have a much fuller picture of Ann's views on gender. It's not hard, when you take a glance at Ann's completed Identity Zone chart, to see why she and Robert clashed. Ann is essentially a Heat Wave on this issue (hot, selective, activist, and reformist-transformational). Without going through the full list of indicators, let's make a chart for Robert, too, assuming that he is a Cold Front (cold, selective, passive, and conformist). Now compare their two charts. These two were an accident waiting to happen! If you factor in their differing values on humor and social equality, you begin to see they were almost sure to end up in a zone-based conflict—especially if they hadn't bothered to take note of their zone differences during other interactions.

Of course, it's not always possible to do this kind of in-depth analysis in the moment—certainly not during a blowout, when temperatures are running high. But you can learn to do an "on-the-spot" zone check, especially if you know the individual or individuals involved. Robert and the rest of our team knew enough about each other that evening to gather a snapshot that would have helped them avoid the blowout, or at least ratchet down the tension.

ROBERT: ALL ZONES
AFFILIATION: GENDER

Temperature	Hot	Warm	Cold
Circle of Inclusion	Closed	Selective	Open
Commitment	Activist	Engaged	Passive
Strategy	Transform	Reform	Conform
Power	High	Medium	Low

ANN: ALL ZONES
AFFILIATION: GENDER

Temperature	Hot	Warm	Cold
Circle of Inclusion	Closed	Selective	Open
Commitment	Activist	Engaged	Passive
Strategy	Transform	Reform	Conform
Power	High	Medium	Low

Adjusting Your Telescope

You can't read others effectively until you really know yourself. That's why I started the book with part 2, titled—yes—"Knowing Yourself." Before you try to read other people's Identity Zones, you should be highly attuned to your affiliations and values, your zots, your blind spots, weaknesses, biases, and so forth. This sensitivity and perception, practiced within, will inevitably help you with another person.

This is especially important when you start examining people's zones, which are expressed on a continuum, as a matter of degrees. Picture your own place on the continuum as a literal place: one of a thousand little islands, all surrounded by water and sky. You're stuck on the beach, peering through a telescope across the vast sea, trying to focus on all the other islands. But the islands you see are unclear; your own zones act as a filter, changing what you see, distorting some things, and bringing others into sharp focus.

Reading people's Identity Zones is a subjective process, not an objective one, because we're all stuck on our own islands. When you try to assess a zone dynamic, check your work frequently. Your place within the zone continuum might skew your perspective. You need to ask yourself:

Am I more extreme than I think? We sometimes place ourselves in the middle of the zone continuum because we like the idea of being moderate. Try to be more honest with yourself. Do you frequently judge others harshly on a particular affiliation or value? If you sometimes feel like everyone around you is a traitor to the cause, colluding with the enemy and selling out—well, you're more activist than merely engaged. If you feel like everyone's always flying off the handle, letting their emotions run away with them, you could be cold rather than warm. If you think others are always playing the victim, not standing up for their rights, your perceived power could be greater than you first realized. And so on.

Am I clear about my priorities? In part 2, we prioritized your affiliations and values. I also said you would have the opportunity to go back and reconsider your list. This is one of those times. If you've found yourself butting heads over and over with certain people—and you don't know why—perhaps there's an unacknowledged affiliation or value at play. If you're surprised by how judgmental you can be, you may be processing a life change that has you hotter, more activist, more closed, et cetera. Remember how Dana, the new parent, found herself dismissing parents on the cold side of the continuum? She saw them as clueless or uncaring drones. Realizing this helped Dana to understand how parental status had shifted into a high-priority affiliation for her.

Am I seeing strengths and weaknesses clearly? When individuals or groups stand on opposite sides of the zone continuum, they tend to get locked into negative views of each other.

People who are hot tend to judge people who are cold by their weaknesses, not their strengths. In the Chicken Wing Incident, that's how Ann saw Robert—as uncaring and unaware. And Robert judged Ann by her weaknesses, too, seeing her as irrational, over the top, consumed by anger. At the dinner party that Gavin and Maria attended, the primary affiliation in play was political affiliation. Once Maria's friends ignored the red flags related to their interaction, Gavin developed an increasingly negative view of their behavior. Gavin thought they were all operating out of their Identity Zone weaknesses and saw them as:

- Over the top, irrational (temperature)
- Exclusionary and closed-minded (circle of inclusion)
- Intent on changing his mind and proving him wrong (commitment)
- Radical in their solutions (strategy)
- Playing the victim because his/her party wasn't in power (power)

Let's go back to Robert and Ann again. As you review the strength and weakness charts below, imagine how Robert's and Ann's troubles grew as they locked into the negative view of one another, based on the weaknesses of each zone. In truth, they were both capable of moving toward their strengths, rather than their weaknesses—but only if one of them was willing to give the other just a little more credit. Ultimately, their mutual negativity created a self-fulfilling prophecy for them.

TEMPERATURE ZONE: COLD
STRENGTHS AND WEAKNESSES

Zone 1: Temperature Cold Strengths	Zone 1: Temperature Cold Weaknesses
• Objectivity • Focusing on practical solutions • Diffusing tension between others • Giving helpful advice on boundaries/social/political • Open to new information • Supporting others who are sensitive • Empathizing with those who are sensitive	• Unaware of issues • Fear of engaging • Condescending • Defensiveness • Not expressing empathy • Moving too quickly to problem-solving mode • Dismissing or overlooking problems • Using inappropriate humor • Avoiding/suppressing discussion

TEMPERATURE ZONE: HOT
STRENGTHS AND WEAKNESSES

Zone 1: Temperature Hot Strengths	Zone 1: Temperature Hot Weaknesses
• Voicing the need for increased sensitivity • Standing up for your beliefs • Demanding respect from others • Refusing to tolerate injustice • Challenging authority/status quo • Giving constructive feedback to others • Supporting or speaking up for others	• Ranting and Raving • Overly Confrontational • Closed and Defensive • Resorting to aggression/violence • Undermining/slandering/de-faming others • Punishing others through emotional, physical, or spiritual withdrawal • Knee-jerk reactions • Inflexibility

How Group Dynamics Impact Conflict

How would the Chicken Wing Incident play out differently if Robert and Ann were alone, without supporting players to influence their behavior? Robert might have been less interested in finding an audience for his humorous comments; Ann might have sought another, more persuasive way to engage Robert on the issue, digging deeper without escalating the conflict to the level of sweeping, systemic change.

To Robert, our choice of restaurants was simple. When he first looked through his telescope, all he saw were the best chicken wings in town. To Ann, on the other hand, our choice was full of significance. She pointed her telescope at the rest of us, looking for support, empathy, and understanding. To meet her expectations, we needed to express at least some of the following:

- An appropriately indignant, offended response (temperature)
- Confirmation that the group deserved her personal and professional respect and trust (circle of inclusion)
- Willingness to take a stand against the subjugation/denigration/exploitation of women (commitment)
- Willingness to examine and take steps to change any underlying systemic problems related to gender issues in our professional group (strategy)
- Support for women who stand up to men in power (personal and situational/hierarchal power)
- An awareness of the historic fight for women's rights and the ongoing fight against socially sanctioned sexism (societal power)

There's much more to be said about group dynamics, especially as they affect organizations, communities, and societies, even countries. I recently introduced the Identity Zones framework to a group of seven managers at a consulting firm. They asked if the framework could be used to better understand global politics and conflicting American views about our role in the international arena. We discussed how affiliations, values, and Identity Zones inform our views of today's world, especially in the wake of the 9/11 terrorist attacks, the war in Iraq, and a global assault on terrorism.

How can we, as Americans, come to consensus about our *national identity* in this new world? I challenged the managers to answer this question for themselves. To begin, I had each of them consider the United States as a whole. Using the affiliation of nationality, could they create an Identity Zones chart for the whole country? Could they "read" the nation in this way? We decided on a participative—if unscientific—approach: we would each produce our own charts, then stack them all together to create a blended portrait, based on the average reading for each zone.

As we created and revealed our individual charts, there was surprisingly little variance. The portrait of the United States that emerged from the seven charts was as follows:

- Temperature: between *warm* and *hot* on nationality
- Circle of Inclusion: charted *selective* on nationality
- Commitment: between *activist* and *engaged* on nationality
- Strategy: between *transformational* and *reformist* on nationality
- Power: between *moderate* and *high* on nationality

UNITED STATES
AFFILIATION: NATIONALITY

Temperature	Hot	Warm	Cold
Circle of Inclusion	Closed	Selective	Open
Commitment	Activist	Engaged	Passive
Strategy	Transform	Reform	Conform
Power	High	Medium	Low

We studied our portrait and discussed it further. We agreed that we were looking at a nation in the grips of a heat wave—highly sensitive, highly committed, and pushing for change on issues related to nationality. Soon, however, it also became clear that we were looking at the same issues from two different sides of a philosophical fence. Some supported the present international policy of our government, and others were decidedly against it. Our exercise revealed a more deeply divided country than we thought.

While analyzing the chart, one of the managers in the room astutely recognized that there were also conflicting values at play in our national debates. We identified some of them as patriotism, world peace, cooperation, loyalty, authority, and integrity.

The managers were able to identify certain triggers that inspire debate within the country on nationality. Depending on your personal views, these triggers may provoke a different response.

- Criticism from other countries about U.S. policies and use of military power
- New limitations on immigrants, foreign students, and tourists
- Changing national, state, and city policies to avert terrorist attacks and implement evacuation strategies and preparedness procedures
- New international policies (for example, preemptive strikes)
- Use of our superpower status to produce a desired outcome

Going Beyond "Win or Lose" Thinking

Because I was speaking to a group of managers, I felt it was important to guide our discussion back toward their roles as leaders. I asked, "What would you do if you were a mediator, charged with bringing the people of the United States together to engage in civil discourse about our differing perspectives?" I asked them to consider opposing camps, both acting as heat waves on the same issue. Here are a few of the things they said during their analysis:

Reinforce Superordinate Values. Reinforce first principles, such as freedom of speech and the right to disagree. Remind the country that our ability to disagree civilly is what makes our country great.

Focus on Civil Society. Strengthen our sense of community and interconnectedness during divisive times.

Stop Demonizing the Other Side. Such tactics will only deepen the conflict and create bitter wounds that will not easily heal after the crisis.

Stop Sensationalizing. Distorting the nature of our arguments to make our points more dramatically only serves to ratchet up the tension and conflict. In a 24/7 news and information world, presenting the issues in a dignified and responsible manner can contribute to a positive tone.

Analyze the Deeper Issues. Work to create solidarity with other nations that share our dilemma. Examine potential lessons to be learned about how and why we are engaged in this struggle. Go beyond sound bites and defensiveness and blame. Acknowledge and accept complex legacies and root causes.

Listen to and Engage the Middle. If ever there were a time for the warm, selective, engaged, reformers to make their voice heard, it's now. Far too much attention is paid to the loud noise. People who can understand both perspectives and serve as a bridge need to step up, and when they do we need to respect their moderation.

The web of community is powerful. Each interaction we have contributes to the overall tone, feel, and vibe. Will we contribute positively? Will we reject divisiveness, short-term thinking, and one-dimensional analysis? Will we stop framing everything according to us versus them, might versus right, and win-lose propositions? Will we stop pushing zots on purpose? Can we remember to focus on shared values?

The dynamics of countries are essentially similar to the dynamics of any large group of people with a leadership structure—companies, schools, community organizations, etcetera. Both leaders and individuals must find a collective approach that brings out all the strengths of the zone continuum.

Exercise: Group Dynamics

Chose a group setting such as your workplace, community, social organization, religious institution, or school. Now, select a value or affiliation and decide where *clusters* of people fall within the chart. It helps to think about clusters of people by level. How will senior people fall in the chart relative to more junior people? How will people in one department fall relative to those in another department? How will job functions, responsibilities, or duties affect where clusters fall? (Of course, you can always start by charting men and women.)

After you have completed your chart, think about where you would fall. You may want to answer some or all of the following questions to analyze your chart:

- Are people acting out of the strengths or weaknesses of their zone placement?

- How are the interactions affecting the overall tone of the environment?
- What impact do you see in the effectiveness of the environment based on your zone placement?
- What kind of changes could move people toward the strengths of the zones—and improve the environment?

Temperature	Hot	Warm	Cold
Circle of Inclusion	Closed	Selective	Open
Commitment	Activist	Engaged	Passive
Strategy	Transform	Reform	Conform
Power	High	Medium	Low

Exercise: Charting Your Relationship

Now I want you to jump in and begin to use your knowledge from this section of the book to gather information and chart a relationship. To do this, you should choose a relationship in which you are experiencing zone-based conflict. The better you know the person, the more complete you will be able to make your chart. Here is the five-step process I'd like you to use:

1. Following the instructions on pages 115–116, complete the domain/investment and risk/reward charts below. This will help you place the relationship in context, understanding the nature of your connection and your level of investment.

High Risk ————————————— Low Risk

High Reward ————————————— Low Reward

2. Next, determine the primary affiliations and/or values that underlie the challenges in your selected relationship. To do this, you may want to review the following from the exercises in part 2:

Your list of affiliations
Your list of values
The red flags that you identified

3. Next, chart yourself on one of the values/affiliations you identified. (Refer to the charting process in part 2).

4. Now do your best to complete a chart for the person you selected, and "stack" it on top of your own. If you're not sure about some of the indicators, take your best guess or simply leave that zone blank. Make sure you mark your choices and the other person's choices in different colors, so that they remain distinct. (You can review the process of stacking charts in chapter 9).

5. Review the strengths and weaknesses charts in chapters 4–8 and try to "adjust your telescope." Are you viewing your relationship clearly? Are you compensating for your blind spots? Are you judging the other more stringently because you're a heat wave or cold front?

I hope this completed chart will give you some added insights into your selected relationship. Remember, we are not really solving problems or fixing anything quite yet; we just want to better understand what's going on. If you choose to take action, the next part of the book, "Crossing Zones," will provide you with useful tools and strategies.

Temperature	Hot	Warm	Cold
Circle of Inclusion	Closed	Selective	Open
Commitment	Activist	Engaged	Passive
Strategy	Transform	Reform	Conform
Power	High	Medium	Low

Part 4

CROSSING THE ZONES

Peace is not merely the absence of war. It is also a state of mind. Lasting peace can come only to peaceful people.

—Jawaharlal Nehru (1889–1964)

Up to this point we've focused primarily on using the Identity Zones framework as an analytical tool, to understand yourself and your relationships. Along the way I've suggested some behaviors and strategies that you can use to avoid inflaming tensions and triggering blowouts. Now I want to elaborate, taking the concepts we've discussed and using them practically—turning them into real behavioral methods. I like to think of these methods as "crossing zones." What's the safest way to cross a busy intersection of competing affiliations, values, and Identity Zones? I hope that after you read this part of the book, you'll feel more comfortable navigating today's multiworld. Perhaps, as the above quote suggests, you will begin to think differently about your interactions, achieving a state of mind that leads to compromise, to productive discussion, to a more peaceful existence.

Let's use my relationship with Luke, my eleven-year-old son, in order to get started. Luke and I constantly engage in debates that will seem familiar to other parents, usually concerning what he can and cannot do. He accuses me of being unfair; I tell him that he is being unrealistic.

Our latest bouts have centered on two topics: his desire for a motorcycle dirt bike, and his ability to stay at home alone without a babysitter. The fact that I am clearly opposed to both (and that, until recently, I've been unwilling to negotiate the terms) seems, to him, a sign of my overprotective nature. He thinks that Laurie and I put limitations on him that none of his other friends have, and we never let him have anything that he really wants. On more than one occasion, he has accused me of treating him "like a baby."

From my perspective, however, Luke doesn't understand the real risks associated with his desires. I have carefully assessed his readiness to handle more responsibility and think he still has a way to go. In addition, it bothers me that Luke focuses on what he *doesn't* have, rather than on the many, many things he has. Luke's lack of appreciation for his relatively privileged life triggers my zot on socioeconomic status. To me, it seems like Luke always wants something newer, better, bigger. Our discussions about what he "needs" have escalated into tense interactions over the past year. Finally, I decided to put my current work into practice—to use the Identity Zones framework to defuse the situation before it grew more chronic and detrimental to us all.

First, I gathered information. I talked with Laurie to get her perspective. I talked to other parents of preadolescents, too, and found that my experience was not uncommon. I began to understand my goal here: to show Luke my respect and love without being goaded into a bad decision for my son's future. I saw that the primary affiliations involved were socioeconomic status for me, and age for him. Competing values were autonomy, independence, and fitting in for Luke, and security and responsibility for me.

Going deeper with my diagnosis, I began to see that the conflict was playing out in the following zones:

- **Temperature.** If you're the parent of an adolescent, you've probably found, like me, that your temperature *rises* when it comes to your child, because your level of investment is so high. I have to remind myself that my son is at a critical juncture in his life, forging an identity separate from his family, struggling to understand himself and his place in the world. No wonder questions of identity evoke such strong feelings! Luke and I clash on these issues because each of us is extremely sensitive about the competing values/affiliations at play. I am warm-hot on socioeconomic status, security, and responsibility. He is hot on autonomy, independence, and age.
- **Strategy.** A family is a system, with its own formal and informal rules and norms, just like any community group or corporation. Luke wants major reforms within the system—he wants us to change the rules to give him more freedom and responsibility. Laurie and I felt the rules we had established were sound. But after reflecting on Luke's feelings, we have decided that we are open to some gradual, modest reforms, which I will detail in a moment.

- **Power.** We have learned how power dynamics can have an impact on the nature of a relationship. Parent–child is one of those relationships with an inherent imbalance of power. Not only do I have the power to tell Luke what he can or cannot do, but I also wield financial power over him. My arguments with Luke are intense because Luke feels *disempowered* at the exact moment in his life when he craves more autonomy. For him to obtain a dirt bike, a symbol of autonomy and freedom, he needs me to give him both money and permission.

Luke's strong values (autonomy, freedom from his parents, the desire to relax or suspend limiting rules, fitting in with his friends) are certainly age appropriate. But because he does not have the power to act on them without our permission, he is "stuck" in conformist mode against his will. Not surprisingly, this has frustrated him. Over time, as his frustration built, he began acting out of his zone weaknesses. When he operated through these weaknesses, his behavior triggered me—then I began to operate out of my own zone weaknesses. It was a vicious cycle, and it took time and effort to understand what was really going on between us.

First, I had to accept the inevitable: we weren't going to stop triggering each other's zots. We were struggling with a zone-based conflict in the family domain, in an intimate relationship with a high level of investment. The first step when we're crossing zones is to acknowledge that we can't "fix" every disagreement. This is especially true in close relationships. Sometimes we get triggered, sometimes we trigger. Sometimes we get angry and fly off the handle. Sometimes we slow down and respond thoughtfully and deliberately. Sometimes we argue, debate, discuss. Sometimes we punish through silence, or we cry because our feelings are hurt. Sometimes we have meaningful discussions. Sometimes we have blowouts.

All of the above are true in my relationship with Luke. After accepting that our zone-based conflict was not going to be solved overnight, I decided to focus on some concrete steps to improve communication and change the destructive patterns that were damaging our relationship. Most urgently, I felt I needed to change my own behavior in the moment. Usually, our disagreements started because I told Luke no. No, he couldn't go out alone with his friends. No, he couldn't have a dirt bike. No, he couldn't have money for whatever new thing all the other kids were buying. I triggered his zots and then he, in turn, triggered mine. I wanted to change this pattern by acknowledging Luke's feelings immediately, showing him respect and understanding when his zots were triggered. My new approach can be summarized as a set of "in the moment" guidelines for what to do when you trigger someone's zots. These are common sense, general guidelines, which can be used with the Zone-by-Zone Guide that follows.

In the moment . . .

- *Ask* what you said or did (why are you upset?).
- *Listen* to the response before you defend your actions.
- *Paraphrase* why you think they are upset.
- *Acknowledge* their feelings about what you said/did.
- *Apologize* for the impact, if appropriate.
- *Share* your intent or perspective, if appropriate.
- *Agree* on a new approach for future interactions, if appropriate.

The "R" Process

It's always best to use time and distance as your ally when you're crossing zones. In long-term relationships, where the level of investment is relatively high, you have time to be thoughtful and deliberate about changing behavior. In addition to the in-the-moment guidelines, I recommend a systematic approach I call the R Process. You can use this along with the dos and don'ts in the Zone-by-Zone guide that follows. It could take days, weeks, months to move through each step of the R Process. You may cycle back through the steps over and over again as you gain new understanding of the zone dynamics of your relationship. I'll share with you some of the choices Laurie, Luke, and I made.

RETREAT to get distance and think about the conflict. After one of our blowouts with Luke, Laurie and I spent about an hour discussing how often the dirt bike had come up lately. Finally, we agreed that we needed to come up with a solution—a compromise that would work for all of us, that would take his feelings into account without sacrificing our concerns about safety and reasonable limits. Laurie suggested that we set a date for a discussion about the dirt bike. In the meantime, we asked Luke to agree not to raise the issue.

REWIND and look for red flags/zots in past interactions. We went back and catalogued all the recent arguments we'd had about the dirt bike. Together, we realized that Luke was focused less on the dirt bike than on what his other friends were doing. He had friends who were walking to school alone and going to movies alone, for example, in addition to riding dirt bikes. By rewinding, we were able to find the common theme in each of our discussions. We saw that every time the dirt bike came up, we triggered Luke's zots on some key values and affiliations: freedom, autonomy, and age.

REFLECT on patterns of behavior. Once we rewound, we began to see how we were getting "hooked" on the wrong things. We stopped seeing the dirt bike as merely an expensive, dangerous toy. We saw it clearly as a symbol. He was undergoing an identity shift, placing a new value on freedom and autonomy, and he saw us as "stuck" in outdated views about responsibility, security, and safety.

RISK taking action. If you're not sure whether you're ready, create a domain/investment chart and risk/reward continuum for the relationship (See Chapter 12).

REPORT your perspective. If you decide it's worth the risk, it's time to share your insights about the situation with the other person in as nonjudgmental a way as possible. Laurie and I set a date with Luke for our discussion. We shared our concerns about the dirt bike; we gave him all of our reasons about safety, cost, and responsibility. We made it clear that we weren't comfortable buying him a dirt bike yet.

REQUEST that you and the other person do things differently. Although we weren't prepared to buy Luke a dirt bike, we acknowledged he was getting older and had a new need for autonomy and freedom. We proposed that over the next two years, if he could save half of the cost of the dirt bike, we would help him purchase one when he was thirteen. We added that he needed to do the research to find a place to ride one in our area and convince us that he could use it responsibly. In general, we asked him to think about how, now that he was eleven, he could demonstrate responsibility and maturity. In return, we promised to treat him accordingly.

REACH agreement. Make an agreement on what you will do differently and, if possible, build in some safeguards to monitor this agreement. Luke agreed to our proposal. Then we moved into a new phase of heated discussions about allowances, and his many schemes to earn money. But the tension subsided over the dirt bike, because we took the time to create a proposal that honored all of our feelings and included a measurable goal.

REMIND yourself and others. Don't be surprised if both parties need some reminders about your new understanding. Changing patterns of behavior is difficult. There have been many occasions in which we have had to remind each other about our agreement with Luke. But these discussions are much healthier than the previous blowouts.

Crossing Zones: A Zone-by-Zone Guide

In the following chapters you'll find insights, strategies, and behavioral dos and don'ts that can help you when you're crossing zones. I've included four main categories of information related to each zone continuum:

- **Drivers.** These are the motivators, the core desires behind each place within the zone continuum. Awareness of drivers can help you adjust your behavior and avoid triggering zots.
- **Filters.** Filters are ways of seeing—perspectives or biases. You can see a place on the zone continuum negatively or positively, depending on your own place on the continuum.

- **Dos and Don'ts.** Simply put, dos and don'ts give you specific, behavioral directions that can improve interactions and avoid blowouts.
- **Rapport-Building Strategies.** Use these new techniques once you have established some degree of trust.

14

Temperature

Hot

Driver: "Respect my feelings."

When someone is hot on an affiliation or value, the most important thing you can do is simply respect their feelings. Even if you disagree with their opinions and cannot understand their perspective, don't dismiss them or discount how they feel. Those who are hot really want you to recognize and appreciate the intensity of their feelings.

Filters

If you view someone's behavior through a negative filter, it will be almost impossible for you to honor the driver.

Judgmental/Negative Filter
- Always dumps on others
- Acts irrational, angry, hurt, or afraid

- Intimidates those around them
- Acts aggressively confrontational
- Seems too defensive
- Blames others and denies all responsibility
- Often resorts to aggression and violence
- Undermines, slanders, or defames others
- Demonstrates passive-aggressive behavior
- Shuts down emotionally
- Offers knee-jerk liberalism/conservatism

Viewing behavior through a positive filter, however, makes it easier for you to use the driver and improve communication.

Sympathetic/Positive Filter:
- Freely expressing real anger, pain, fear
- Standing up for their beliefs
- Demanding respect
- Refusing to tolerate injustice
- Challenging the status quo
- Offering constructive feedback
- Speaking up for a worthy cause
- Protecting themselves and others from exploitation
- Raising important issues

Sometimes, hot personalities seem irrational—just as cold personalities seem lifeless and uncaring. But you have to make sure that your bias is not so strong, so unconsciously present at all times, that you automatically default to pat interpretations.

Dos and Don'ts

Do . . .
- Acknowledge that you've heard their feelings and you understand how passionately they feel; in fact, you should try to learn more about the experiences that drove them to this passionate belief. This establishes an empathetic environment.

- Serve as an interpreter when they struggle to express their perspective. This further demonstrates your empathy.
- Make sure they can voice their opinions in a group setting, and that they don't get shut down prematurely or drowned out by the crowd; this will help to establish trust.
- Whenever possible, take on some of their burden, so they don't always have to police the actions of others or act as organizational watchdogs. This demonstrates support for their position and validates their concerns—especially if you witness certain behaviors personally.
- Raise volatile topics carefully and strategically, trying your best to avoid unnecessary controversy. This keeps everyone focused on the task at hand.
- Once you have established some rapport, strategize with them about communicating their position effectively; help them open doors, rather than nail them shut.

Don't . . .

- Make jokes that target their hot affiliation/value, especially in a work environment where such humor could have unintended consequences.
- Avoid difficult issues that hot personalities may raise without offering an alternative time/forum for that discussion.
- Tell them they are being oversensitive.
- Minimize or criticize their feelings.
- Tell them that their feelings are wrong or misguided.

Rapport-Building Strategies

- Periodically ask them how they are feeling.
- Ask if they need any support or encouragement on a challenging issue.
- Ensure that the system/organization/group is treating them with respect.
- Request personal feedback of any kind.

Warm

Driver: "Respect my moderation."

When someone is warm on an affiliation or value, the most important action you can take is to respect her moderation. Even if you disagree with her choice, be strategic about when you speak up. What warm personalities want more than anything is the freedom to choose when and where they show the cards in their hand.

Filters

If you view someone's behavior through negative filters, it will be almost impossible for you to honor the driver.

Judgmental/Negative Filter

- Inconsistent
- Wishy-washy
- Not committed
- Unwilling to take a risk
- Standing on both sides of the fence
- Co-opted

Viewing behavior through positive filters, however, makes it easier for you to use the driver and improve communication.

Sympathetic/Positive Filter

- Reasonable
- Strategic
- Selective
- Prioritizing
- Even tempered
- Choosing their battles
- Not sweating the small stuff
- Brokers, peacemakers

Dos and Don'ts

Do . . .

- Let them make up their minds about when they want to support you.
- Express appreciation when they support your perspective.
- Utilize their ability to see both sides.
- Utilize their sense of caution about a situation.
- Utilize them as an intermediary if they agree.

Don't . . .

- Put them on the spot.
- Force them to choose sides.
- Ask them to be more or less than they want to be in any situation.
- Resent the fact that sometimes you will have their support and sometimes you won't.
- Use disparaging terms to describe them (such as "sellout").

Rapport-Building Strategies

- Ask them what else you can do to help them feel more comfortable.
- Define the objective so they can participate in the way that is best for them.
- Ask what the organization or group can do to help them feel that it's okay to step out more.
- Tell them how their leadership and open participation can make a difference.

Cold

Driver: "Respect my right to focus on other priorities."

When someone is cold on an affiliation or value, the most important action you can take is to respect their right to focus on other priorities—

even if you disagree with their choice. What Cold personalities want more than anything is the right to decide what is important to them.

Filters

If you view behavior through negative filters, it will be almost impossible for you to honor the driver.

Judgmental/Negative Filter

- Indifferent, unfeeling, or disconnected
- Unaware
- Withdrawn
- Afraid
- Condescending
- Patronizing
- Contemptuous
- Defensive
- Not expressing empathy
- Moving too quickly to problem-solving mode
- Dismissing or overlooking
- Blocking the investment of time or resources
- Avoiding debate or discussion
- Undermining/slandering/defaming others ("they're out of control")

Viewing behavior through positive filters, however, makes it easier for you to use the driver and improve communication.

Sympathetic/Positive Filter

- Rational or logical
- Analytical
- Objective
- Keeping perspective
- Focusing on practical solutions
- Diffusing tensions and conflicts among others

- Prioritizing
- Giving advice on boundaries/social/political norms
- Uninformed/unfamiliar with issues

Remember to make sure that your bias is not so strong and operating so unconsciously that you automatically default to any of these interpretations.

Dos and Don'ts

Do . . .

- Allow them space to be personally disengaged. When they have more time to think about your perspective they may be better prepared to have a discussion.
- Acknowledge and respect their right to be personally disengaged (cold) but, if appropriate, define specifically what they need to do in their job or other role to respond to others' sensitivities.
- Give them a clear reason to be more engaged and invested if you need their help.

Don't . . .

- Make jokes related to their insensitivity or "heartlessness."
- Use phrases like, "they just don't get it."
- Use their detachment as an opportunity to label them as racist, sexist, or any other "ist" without clear behavioral data to support such a claim.
- Lecture, preach, or try to make them change their mind after they have said they don't want to.

Rapport-Building Strategies

- Use them as a sounding board to understand how others who are cold may see the situation.

- Ask them for advice about how to frame the issue in a way that others will hear it.
- Use them as a barometer to avoid shutting others down or out.
- Let them know when they are at risk of being viewed as uninformed or out of touch, which could undermine their effectiveness.

15

Circle of Inclusion

Closed

Driver: "Respect my right to exclude you from my intimate circle."

When someone is closed on an affiliation or value, the most important action you can take is to respect their right to exclude you from their intimate social circle—even if you disagree with their choice. What people who are closed want more than anything is the right to associate with those who share their beliefs and/or life experiences. Of course, this stance has legal implications in the workplace. But whenever and wherever an individual has the legal right to choose, you can reduce tension by respecting that right.

Filters

If you view behavior through negative filters, it will be almost impossible for you to honor the driver.

Judgmental/Negative Filter

- Exclusionary
- Narrow
- Closed-minded
- Prejudiced/biased
- Self-limiting
- Paranoid/afraid
- Plotting
- Distrustful
- Stereotyping others
- Rigid
- Superior/elite attitude
- Maintaining "purity"
- Living in the past
- Superficial

Viewing behavior through positive filters, however, makes it easier for you to use the driver and improve communication.

Sympathetic/Positive Filter

- Proud
- Supporting their own
- Strong values
- Maintaining the integrity or purity of customs and traditions
- Building community
- Empowering their group/cause
- Demonstrating strength in numbers

Dos and Don'ts

Do . . .

- Let them know why their perspective is valuable to you.
- Give them concrete reasons if you want them to be more open; tie your request to an outcome that matters to you, to the team, to the organization, to the community.

- Let them know immediately if their exclusion of others jeopardizes them or your organization in any way.
- Tell them if they are missing a critical perspective or data point before they make an important decision that will affect others.

Don't . . .

- Impose or force yourself in their social environment because you feel left out or it seems unfair.
- Try to "break up" a closed group because you are worried about what they are doing.
- Write them off as unimportant.
- Forget to solicit their opinion or perspective when decisions are made that affect them.

Rapport-Building Strategies

- Emphasize the benefits and values of being more open such as new ideas, fresh perspectives, personal growth, professional growth, more clients, and more votes.
- Try to understand the reason that they are closed (safety, philosophy, politics, etc.).
- Explain why their participation is important.
- Learn as much as you can about their affiliation/value.
- Invite them into your group(s) as a way to build bridges.

Selective

Driver: "Respect my right to pick and choose."

When someone is selective on an affiliation or value, the most important action you can take is to "respect his right to pick and choose"—even if you disagree with how he chooses to form his social circle. What someone who is selective wants more than anything is the right to associate with whomever he chooses, *based on his own criteria.*

Filters

If you view behavior through negative filters, it will be almost impossible for you to honor the driver.

Judgmental/Negative Filter

- One foot in, one foot out
- Inconsistent
- Trying to have it both ways
- Forcing you and others to assimilate in order to get in
- A token

Viewing behavior through positive filters, however, makes it easier for you to use the driver and improve communication.

Sympathetic/Positive Filter

- A possible bridge
- Fair
- Making choices based on individual circumstances
- Open to change, but holding onto core identity

Dos and Don'ts

Do . . .

- Respect their ability to see many sides.
- Take advantage of their ability to honor their base and expand beyond it.
- Utilize them as bridge builders.
- Utilize them to understand the realistic challenges.

Don't . . .

- Put them on the spot.
- Force them to be inclusive.
- Force them to be exclusive.
- Exclude them because they associate with "them."

- Assume that because you've been "let in," that you can use "insider" humor or language.

Rapport-Building Strategies

- Respect their core affiliation or values.
- If they are taking a risk by being selective, honor their willingness to open the circle.
- Sympathize if they feel caught in the middle.
- Demonstrate support for their issues or challenges when you agree.

Open

Driver: "Respect my right to welcome everyone and treat everyone equally."

When people are open on an affiliation or value, the most important action you can take is to respect their right to associate with whomever they want—even if you disagree with their choices. What someone who is open wants more than anything is the right to associate with people regardless of whether they share this affiliation/value.

Filters

If you view behavior through negative filters, it will be almost impossible for you to honor the driver.

Judgmental/Negative Filter

- Naive
- Out of touch with reality
- In denial about problems
- Selling out
- Forgetting who they really are
- Out for themselves

- Without a core or center
- Self-hating
- Without pride
- Abandoning their group
- Better than others
- Opportunistic

Viewing behavior through positive filters, however, makes it easier for you to use the driver and improve communication.

Sympathetic/Positive Filter

- Available to everyone
- Not prejudiced
- Broad-minded
- Harmonizing
- Fair
- Trusting
- Optimistic
- Curious about others
- Appreciating variety
- Bridging differences
- Leveraging differences
- Not stuck in the past/forward-thinking
- Rising above the superficial

Dos and Don'ts

Do . . .

- Allow them to keep the doors open to others.
- Solicit their ideas on how to create a more trusting inclusive environment.
- Use them to understand some of the agendas and positions that may not be on the table.
- Use them as ambassadors to bridge differences.

- Share with them some of the benefits of being selective (e.g., sometimes limiting participation can increase productivity, governance, and efficiency).
- Give them clear time frames and outcomes and ask them how they will accomplish their goal with all the differences they want to include.
- Help them manage the tensions that arise from multiple perspectives.

Don't . . .

- Call them Pollyannas.
- Call them traitors to their own.
- Tell them they have to choose whose side they're on.
- Tell them they are now one of "them," that they lost their credentials, or forgot where they came from.

Rapport-Building Strategies

- Tap them to get a sense of the vibe of a situation or environment.
- Use them to find resources from a variety of sources.
- Ask them about new people who would be good to add to a team or project.
- Use them to brainstorm solutions that would be accepted across a wide range of people.

16

Strategy

Transformational

Driver: "Respect my right to envision a new reality."

When someone wants to completely transform the system, the most important thing you can do is simply respect her right to promote systemic change. Even if you disagree with her vision and tactics, you cannot dismiss her or discount how she feels. Those who are transformers want you to recognize and appreciate the compelling nature of their vision.

Filters

If you view behavior through negative filters, it will be almost impossible for you to honor the driver.

Judgmental/Negative Filters

- Radical
- Disrespectful/Ingrate

- Anarchist
- Unrealistic
- Off balance
- Scary
- Violent
- Rash
- Myopic
- Crackpot
- Crazy
- Suicidal
- Destroying tradition
- Inhumane/inhuman
- Unnatural
- Irrational
- Impatient/rushing/moving too fast
- Out of touch
- Destroyer-Martyr
- Terrorist

Viewing behavior through positive filters, however, makes it easier for you to use the driver and improve communication.

Sympathetic/Positive Filters

- Visionary
- Introducing new paradigm
- Offering breakthrough thinking
- Unyielding in purpose
- Missionary
- Savior-Martyr
- Warrior/Liberator/Freedom fighter
- Catalyst

Dos and Don'ts

Do . . .

- Respectfully listen to their ideas and their perspectives.
- Acknowledge the depth of their concern for the issue.

- Ask if they are open to hearing the impact of their strategy on others.
- Ask if they are open to hearing additional perspectives or alternative solutions.
- Try to understand how they see the flaws or problems in the current system, or norm, or policy.

Don't . . .

- Shut them down without a dialogue.
- Drive them underground.
- Miss an opportunity to clearly understand what they see as the big problems.
- Invite them to participate on a team without defining the boundaries.
- Let them get started on a project and then pull back or change your mind.
- Define them as crazy, incompetent, or irrational without understanding their worldview.
- Assume they will "let it go" in due time.

Rapport-Building Strategies

- Help them see the importance of building a shared vision.
- Encourage them not to give up on the system, but to exercise patience, find support, and build consensus.
- Explore alternative means to accomplish the same goal.
- Help them problem-solve on how to make their point in a way that does not scare off people who might over time be supportive.
- Help them separate their personal agendas and egos from the underlying issues they are trying to address.
- Help them not to always see people who oppose them as the enemy.

Reformist

Driver: "Respect my right to improve the system."

When someone wants to reform the system, the most important thing you can do is respect his right to make suggestions about how to create change—even if you disagree with his ideas. Reformists want you to recognize and appreciate how the situation would improve if it is updated or adjusted as time goes by.

Filters

If you view behavior through negative filters, it will be almost impossible for you to honor the driver.

Judgmental/Negative Filters

- Moving too fast
- Moving too slow
- An agitator
- Being safe
- Disloyal
- Naive
- Dealing with a symptom
- Making a big deal out of very little

Viewing behavior through positive filters, however, makes it easier for you to use the driver and improve communication.

Sympathetic/Positive Filter

- Challenging/pushing the system
- Not throwing the baby out with the bath water
- Acting as a bridge
- Mediating differences
- Making things better
- Tasking risks
- Working on behalf of their constituents or for everybody
- Trusting the system or situation to do the right thing
- Using the accepted norms for change

Dos and Don'ts

Do . . .

- Respectfully listen to their ideas and their perspectives.
- Acknowledge the depth of their concern for the issue.
- Ask if they are open to hearing the impact of their strategy on others.
- Ask if they are open to hearing additional perspectives or alternative solutions.
- Try to understand how they see the flaws or problems in the current system or norm or policy.

Don't . . .

- Change the rules in midstream.
- Work behind the scene to sabotage their efforts.
- Use the system or rules against them.
- Miss an opportunity to understand what they think is wrong and how they and others are affected.
- Tell them they should be doing more or less.
- Tell them they are embarrassing others like them.
- Dismiss their analyses or concerns.

Rapport-Building Strategies

- Help them be clear about what they see that leads them to conclude that a change is necessary.
- Help them clearly understand how the rules and norms and systems work.
- Help them be realistic about time frames to achieve their desired result.
- Help them be clear about the risk to their own and others' reputations.
- Give them support when and where you can.
- Encourage them to work collaboratively with others.
- Help them to know the right timing and why to consider choosing their battles.

- Be clear about what their bottom line is if all of their desired changes are not going to be implemented.

Conformist

Driver: "Respect my right to protect and honor the norm."

When someone wants to conform, the most important thing you can do is simply respect his right to protect and honor the norm. Even if you disagree with his investment in the status quo, you cannot dismiss him or discount how he feels. Those who are conformers want you to recognize and appreciate the pride and sense of security they feel with the existing system.

Filters

If you view behavior through negative filters, it will be almost impossible for you to honor the driver.

Judgmental/Negative Filters

- Colluders
- Self-serving
- Traitors
- Wimps
- Unfair beneficiaries
- Ineffective
- Tokens
- Scared
- Dangerously out of touch
- Stuck
- Out of step, out of date
- Oppressors

Viewing behavior through positive filters, however, makes it easier for you to use the driver and improve communication.

Sympathetic/Positive Filters

- Stakeholders
- Safe
- Being civil
- Being responsible
- Taking the high road
- Dignified
- Understanding and working within the system
- Upholding the laws and norms
- Respecting established traditions
- Playing by the rules

Dos and Don'ts

Do . . .

- Acknowledge their investment and love of and belief in the current system/structure/norms.
- Allow them to express their pride and optimism in what exists.
- Be clear with them about the need for change.
- Honor what you know is good and can be preserved about the existing system.
- Use them as ambassadors to make transitions and changes easier.
- Incorporate some of their ideas into changes.

Don't . . .

- Denigrate things that are important to them.
- Change things and give them no support to help them understand and adopt the new way.
- Assume that they are no longer valuable because they don't agree with your vision or reform ideas.
- Use negative terms to describe them (old school, old guard, dinosaur).
- Assume that change is always good and that they are always wrong.

Rapport-Building Strategies

- Help them to understand the consequence of not changing or amending or making adjustments.
- Enlist them as the guardians of the new.
- Honor heritage/tradition and acknowledge its importance in getting you to where you are now.
- Help them understand the new opportunities that may emerge from change.

17

Commitment

Activist

Driver: "Respect my mission and sense of calling."

When someone is open on an affiliation or value, the most important action you can take is to respect her mission and sense of calling—even if you disagree with the premise of her cause. What activists want more than anything is for you to respect their commitment and dedication.

Filters

If you view behavior through negative filters, it will be almost impossible for you to honor the driver.

Judgmental/Negative Filters

- In your face
- One note/single focus

- Attacking
- Blaming and shaming
- A hammer that sees everything as a nail
- With us or against us
- Black/white thinking
- Lack of balance
- Irritating
- Too persistent
- Obsessive
- Uptight
- Too serious
- Self-righteous

Viewing behavior through positive filters, however, makes it easier for you to use the driver and improve communication.

Sympathetic Positive Filters:

- Earnest
- Focused
- Inspiring
- Moral
- Selfless
- Generous
- Community focused
- Leaders
- Self-sacrificing of money/time

Dos and Don'ts

Do . . .

- Respectfully listen to their perspective.
- Be clear about other priorities that are more relevant to the situation at hand.
- Be honest with them; tell them where your own commitment lies.
- Set clear guidelines about when/if it is appropriate to air their perspective.

Don't . . .

- Make fun of or belittle their cause.
- Make disparaging comments like, "get a life."
- Start a sentence with "you people."
- Put yourself in a position to be seen as a roadblock.
- Undermine them behind the scenes.
- Join the cause and then grandstand.

Rapport-Building Strategies

- Ask them what you should read, view, or attend in order to learn more about their cause.
- When you experience something that reminds you of their cause and its importance, share it with them.
- Remind them to take care of and nurture themselves.
- If you are sincere, ask if there is a way you can (within limits) support them.
- Help them calibrate their intensity to various audiences so they can be more effective.

Engaged

Driver: "Respect my right to regulate my energy."

When someone is engaged on an affiliation or value, the most important action you can take is to respect his right to regulate his energy—even if you disagree with how he chooses when and where he engages. What people who are engaged want more than anything is to choose the level of energy they want to invest.

Filters

If you view behavior through negative filters, it will be almost impossible for you to honor the driver.

Judgmental/Negative Filters

- Hiding
- Not truly committed
- Afraid
- Inconsistent
- Fair-weathered
- Showing up only when it benefits them
- Safer than the activist
- Hard to read
- Fence-straddling

Viewing behavior through positive filters, however, makes it easier for you to use the driver and improve communications.

Sympathetic/Positive Filters

- Strategic
- Realistic
- Choosing battles wisely
- Balanced
- Exercising judgment and timing
- Keeping priorities straight
- Moderate

Dos and Don'ts

Do . . .

- Appreciate the fact that they can be bridges.
- Ask them to share their wisdom related to both perspectives.
- Coach you and others in recognizing the safety/political issues they see that keep them in the middle.
- Ask what they are willing to do to support you behind the scenes.
- Ask what it would take to get their support.

Don't . . .

- Put them on the spot.
- Tell them they should be doing more or less.

- Shame or embarrass them.
- Compare them negatively to others.
- Lecture them.

Rapport-Building Strategies

- Ask questions and be open to responses, learning how they see the pros and cons, strengths and weaknesses, of a particular situation.
- If you sense that they are bothered by something, but concerned about speaking up, then offer them some support.
- Solicit and utilize their advice and support behind the scenes; do this quietly if they do not want public attention.

Passive

Drivers: "Respect my right to disengage."

When someone is passive on an affiliation or value, the most important action you can take is to respect her right to disengage—even if you disagree with her choice not to expend her energy on certain issues. What people who are passive want more than anything is the right to decide what is important to them, without having others' values forced on them.

Filters

If you view behavior through negative filters, it will be almost impossible for you to honor the driver.

Judgmental/Negative Filters

- Afraid/Cowardly
- Selfish
- Free ride
- Lazy
- Lacking conviction

- Clueless
- Foolish
- Hiding their head in the sand
- In denial
- Irresponsible
- Shirking their responsibility
- Colluding
- Uncaring
- Insensitive
- Weak

Viewing behavior through positive filters, however, makes it easier for you to use the driver and improve communication.

Sympathetic/Positive Filters

- Careful
- Considerate
- Deliberative
- Not rash
- Open slate
- Easygoing
- Not intimidating
- Doing no harm
- Above the fray
- Identifying with you
- Giving you space
- Nonjudgmental
- Doing what's required

Dos and Don'ts

Do . . .

- Tell them how their participation and involvement can benefit them.

- Be clear, if they are required to be more engaged for professional reasons, about how their increased engagement is tied to the mission, goals, and strategies of the organization.
- Use them as a barometer to determine where others are on your issue.
- Help them understand how their lack of engagement is being interpreted by you and/or others.
- Be clear about the consequences if certain issues are left unaddressed/unresolved.

Don't . . .

- Guilt-trip.
- Assume their disengagement is mean spirited.
- Assume they don't understand the issue or are stupid.
- Assume they are too incompetent to do anything.
- Assume that they only care about themselves.
- Accuse them of not caring about you because they won't support your cause.

Rapport-Building Activities

- Tell them how their support could be helpful to you or why their support is important to you.
- Acknowledge their voice on important issues.
- Tell them why their perspective is unique/valuable.
- Show them how the issue affects others and how supporting others will make things better for them, the community, and the organization.

18

Power

High

Driver: "Respect my authority."

When someone perceives himself to have high power, the most important thing you can do is respect his authority—even if you feel the power imbalance is unfair. Those who perceive themselves to be high in power want you to recognize and appreciate their sense of responsibility, their sense of accomplishment, and their ability/right to lead/control.

Filters

If you view behavior through negative filters, it will be almost impossible for you to honor the driver.

Judgmental/Negative Filters

- Arrogant
- Controlling

- Manipulative
- Power hungry, power mongering
- Cruel
- Exploiting others
- Maniacal
- Using intimidation tactics
- Evil
- Oppressive
- Holds all the cards
- Out of touch
- Undeserving
- Machiavellian
- Narcissistic
- Paternalistic
- Pompous

Viewing behavior through positive filters, however, makes it easier for you to use the driver and improve communication.

Sympathetic/Positive Filters

- Strong leaders
- Charismatic
- Persuasive
- Inspiring
- Making things happen
- Influential
- In charge
- Courageous
- Determined
- Overcoming adversity
- Effective
- Protecting and benefiting others
- Born to lead
- Blessed

Dos and Don'ts

Do . . .

- Acknowledge their sense of responsibility and the challenges they face.
- Ask for their input and perspective.
- When appropriate, ask for their permission.
- Suggest that if they compromise on some issues, they may have less to manage on some issues.
- When appropriate, follow their rules and preferences to demonstrate your respect and loyalty.
- Make suggestions for power sharing or changes in leadership that don't threaten their position.
- Alert them to ways that the misuse of their power could have a long term detrimental impact on their relationship with others.

Don't . . .

- Challenge/embarrass or take them on publicly without a plan.
- Gripe, slander, or denigrate them behind their backs.
- Assume that they will not listen to your perspective.
- Assume it's easy to hold all the cards.
- Underestimate their stress level.
- Take sides against them without support.
- Assume that they hold *all* of the power.
- Underestimate how important loyalty and willingness to sacrifice are to them.

Rapport-Building Strategies

- Ask how you can help to alleviate some of the burden of responsibility.
- Make suggestions about how more participatory and democratic processes increase commitment, investment, and loyalty.
- Point out times that others are ready to take more responsibility.
- Share your perceptive about how your relationship can be damaged if they always have to have control.

Medium

Driver: "Respect my right to use my power judiciously."

When someone perceives herself to have moderate power, the most important thing you can do is respect her right to use it judiciously—even if you think sometimes she is too cautious or too heavy-handed. Those who perceive themselves to have moderate power want you to recognize and appreciate that they do not hold all of the cards, and they must use their power selectively.

Filters

If you view behavior through negative filters, it will be almost impossible for you to honor the driver.

Judgmental/Negative Filters

- A cog in the wheel
- Limited
- Constrained
- Not confident
- Stuck in the middle
- Frustrated
- Only going so far
- Falling short
- Hitting walls
- Stuck beneath the glass ceiling
- Overreaching
- Out of their league
- Self-serving
- Selling out to gain favor with those who have more power
- Selling out to gain favor with those who have less power
- Challenging you
- Threatening
- A potential adversary
- Adverse to risk
- Hard to read

Viewing behavior through positive filters, however, makes it easier for you to use the driver and improve communication.

Sympathetic/Positive Filters

- Some degree of influence
- Some degree of support
- A range of choices
- Holding some of the cards
- A potential power broker or go-between
- Strategically marshaling and deploying power
- Influential with others who have power
- Able to influence the grass roots
- Able to bring together both and all sides
- Leveraging resources
- Channeling power

Dos and Don'ts

Do . . .

- Acknowledge that they do not have all the authority to control their environment.
- Acknowledge that they have to make strategic choices about how to use the power they have.
- If you support their position, join them so you have more power.
- Use them to assess the risk of exercising power/challenging power.
- Inform them when their support could swing the balance of power.
- Remind them of the influence they have.
- When appropriate, let/encourage them to lead or take charge.

Don't . . .

- Expect them to carry the full weight of a cause or position.
- Expect them always to support you on everything, just because they supported you once.
- Put them on the spot.
- "Set them up" by pretending to have their endorsement.

- Let them take the fall.
- Assume that they don't have a strong idea or position on a topic because they don't choose to speak up.
- Expect them to "spend" their limited power to help you.
- Assume they are aware of the power they have.

Rapport-Building Strategies

- Help them make sure they are not over- or underestimating their power.
- Help them use their power to have an impact on their high-priority affiliations/values.
- Help them to be clear when their use of power can make a positive difference to others.
- Support them when they take risks by exercising more power.

Low

Driver: "Respect my desire to be treated fairly."

When people perceive themselves as having low power, the most important thing you can do is respect their desire to be treated fairly—even if you disagree with their assessment of their power level and their treatment by others. People with low perceived power want you to recognize and appreciate their sense that they've been overlooked or mistreated; they also want more ability to control their destiny on high-priority affiliations/values.

Filters

If you view behavior through negative filters, it will be almost impossible for you to honor the driver.

Judgmental/Negative Filters

- Playing the victim
- Looking for handouts

- Waiting to be saved
- Blaming others
- Dependent
- Pitiable
- Lacking self-respect
- Guilt-inducing
- Afraid to stand up for themselves
- Stuck
- Lazy/not applying themselves
- Ungrateful
- Whiny

Viewing behavior through positive filters, however, makes it easier for you to use the driver and improve communication.

Sympathetic/Positive Filters

- Innocent
- Taken advantage of
- Deserving sympathy
- Needing support
- Powerless
- Victim of circumstances
- Discriminated against
- Underdogs
- Oppressed
- Underrepresented

Dos and Don'ts

Do . . .

- Invite them into the decision-making process when appropriate.
- Ask them what their experience and perspective is.
- Give voice to their perspective and needs when you have more power.
- Champion their right to improve their situation.
- Mentor, guide, teach, and share resources.

- Learn about the level of pain and frustration they feel in their lives.
- Provide growth and empowerment opportunities.

Don't . . .
- Assume that it is safe/easy to seek/exhibit more power.
- Assume that they are not trying or applying themselves.
- Give them more responsibility than they can handle in an attempt to be fair-minded.
- Take it personally if they challenge you or accuse you of not being fair.
- Expect that they will express gratitude for all you've done.
- Keep them in a dependent position because you think they can not take care of themselves.
- Blame them for circumstances that are beyond their control.

Rapport-Building Strategies

- Over time, try to understand the impact that their power perspective has had on their self-esteem, their sense of hope, and their attitude toward risk taking.
- Encourage them to take small steps to prove to themselves that they can handle risky situations.
- Be an ally.
- Help them to find other allies by not always blaming/hating those in power.
- Help them to recognize situations in which they have more power than they think.
- Help them think creatively about alternative ways to exercise more power and control, such as joining with others or seeking group or organizational support.

19

Watch Your Responses

How to Respond When You've Been Triggered

When you're the one who's zots get triggered, your challenge is to act based on the strengths of your Identity Zones, not the weaknesses. Acting from your weaknesses is damaging to the relationship. Ultimately, it's also self-defeating because it insulates you from personal growth, positive change, and achieving your goal within the relationship.

I recently attended a forum on diversity at my sons' school. The forum brought together parents, teachers, and administrators to address a complex issue that most American schools are struggling to manage. The parents sat together in the auditorium while administrators, onstage, responded to a set of prepared questions about their cross-cultural philosophy and approach. They addressed challenges such as disparities in the discipline, retention, and expulsion rates among various cultural groups; teacher and curriculum development; mentoring and support; and testing methodologies. At the end of the session, one of the head administrators said, by way of wrapping up, "I love this kind of dialogue."

A parent spoke up: "I am very pleased with your responses. It seems to me that there is no real problem at our school, based on what I heard tonight. You've thought about almost everything."

I felt like I was going to burst into flames right there in the auditorium. Dialogue! What dialogue? What made this a forum? At no point had the parents been given the opportunity to ask questions of our own. The administrator's answers struck me as too easy, too pat, too obviously prepared in advance. The school claimed to care deeply about diversity, but where was the evidence? What were they really doing to make a difference? How could they possibly stimulate change if they weren't willing to answer tough questions from the front lines—the community whose children were struggling day-to-day with diversity issues?

Their commitment on race was high (they were committed to creating committees, forums, and policies to promote the value of cultural diversity). But their strategy, in my view, fell somewhere between conformist and reformist, whereas mine fell somewhere between reformist and transformational. And, in the Power Zone, I felt frustrated and unfairly treated, without a voice in the dialogue, because it seemed like they had all the situational/hierarchal power (because they were controlling the forum) and I had almost none (because I had no control over the forum).

In the auditorium that evening, all I saw were weaknesses: people too afraid, too stuck in their old ways, too bound by tradition and convention. What I wanted was evidence that they were going to fundamentally change the system: overhaul the curriculum, change the recruiting methods and salary structures for teachers, and create a new school that reflected the new realities. To me, in full transformational mode, it seemed the format of the forum was preventing real dialogue and meaningful change from occurring. When I heard an administrator refer to what had happened that night as a dialogue, I felt a well of resentment bubbling over. My feelings could be summed up like this:

- Too much "dialogue," not enough action! How typical!
- The school is behind the times. They're never going to change.

- It's going to take a full-scale revolt for them to really take action and solve the problems from the ground up.

Well, I didn't start a revolution. But, at that moment, I wanted to. Even after I had cooled down, the event left me with a sense of lingering anger, dissatisfaction, and resentment. Triggers are powerful. Triggers are catalysts. They cause anger, tension, inflamed zots. Triggers can be words, actions, or events. Depending on the context, a trigger can be the thing that first pushed a relationship toward conflict, or the thing that turned a simmering conflict into a blowout.

When you get triggered, one of the ways to keep the tension from escalating is to move from defensive mode to productive mode. I was in defensive mode right after the incident at my sons' school. Nothing productive was going to happen until I took a deep breath, unpacked the situation, and reflected on strategies for moving forward. Below are some examples of defensive and productive responses.

Defensive responses

- Self-righteous: unwilling to see the humanity of the other
- Uni-minded: focused on a single interpretation of the triggering event; refusing to hear the other's perspective
- Acting as judge and jury: assuming negative intent and meting out punishment
- Writing people off: assuming they can't change
- Intimidating through anger: raising the emotional level to the point that people are afraid to take you on
- Stuck in a closed loop: only getting feedback about your opinion/behavior from those in your zone or "on your side"
- Sabotaging: working behind the scenes to undermine the person or organization without giving direct feedback
- Delivering ultimatums: assuming a "take it or leave it" stance that closes down communication and compromise
- Guilt-tripping: using guilt as a vehicle to control
- Stoking the fire: provoking a blowout by deliberately exaggerating, making false accusations, or pulling others into the conflict

Productive responses

- Self-aware: reading the situation to know why you were triggered and how it impacted you
- Illuminating: clearly describing why you were triggered and how it impacted you
- Multiminded: asking for the other's interpretation, perspective, or point of view
- Giving people a chance: remaining open to the possibility that they can change their behavior
- Taking the high road: admitting your weaknesses
- Focusing on outcomes: rejecting revenge and punishment; pursuing your goal for this relationship
- Bridging differences: using shared affiliations, values, and Identity Zones to turn "enemies" into allies
- Forgiving: absolving the other of guilt so it doesn't cloud the issues
- Meeting in the middle: finding a mediator or neutral environment so you can work out a compromise
- Dousing the fire: putting your feelings into perspective; refusing to spiral out of control or get pulled into a blowout

When You Trigger Others

If we're honest with ourselves, we admit that from time to time we trigger zots on purpose. If you're thinking, "not me," consider your relationships in all domains, especially your family. I have a friend whose sister is a struggling artist. My friend lives in New York. His sister lives in Charlottesville, Virginia. Nothing "gets her goat" more than stories about wealthy, celebrated New York artists who, in her opinion, don't deserve their success.

She's hot on regional affiliation and hot on recognition/acclaim. My friend is aware of his sister's sensitivities, but he just can't help himself: when he visits his sister in Charlottesville, he always finds himself telling stories about painters or sculptors who have hit the big time in Manhattan.

Like so many brothers and sisters, their relationship is loving, but they still have a tendency to revert to petty push-pull patterns that trace to childhood.

When you've triggered someone, evaluate whether you did it because you were:

- Unaware of the zots and/or the consequences of your behavior (because you don't know the person, didn't see red flags, never received direct feedback).
- Unconcerned about the person's response (because you didn't care enough about the relationship to avoid the trigger).
- Angry (because you're in conflict, because you were triggered first, because you had a knee-jerk response).
- Stuck in a counterproductive pattern (in a relationship where triggering is part of a "script" you've been following for days, months, or years).
- Joking with good or bad intent (genuinely trying to reach out and lighten up the tension *or* trying to undermine/discredit through humor).
- Looking for shock value (following the example of talk-show hosts, comedians, and others).
- Politicking (using triggers to motivate people around certain issues such as affirmative action, welfare, or Medicare).

In the Chicken Wing Incident, Robert was initially *unaware* that he was triggering Ann's zot on gender. Later, though, as Robert's awareness increased, he tried to use *joking* as a way to smooth over the confrontation, and possibly to subtly discredit her views, which he didn't understand. Over time, through soul-searching, Robert might ask himself if he is limiting his consulting practice in any way—does he have tendency to trigger women on gender issues? He might come to recognize that although humor usually works for him as a way to make people feel at ease, in certain situations it has the opposite effect.

Soul-searching can lead to transformational change, but you must be honest with yourself and remain open to direct and indirect feedback from your environment. Also, remember, this list is useful primarily for looking at *yourself*. If you're trying to make guesses about other people's motivations, you're in dangerous territory. It's much too easy to act as judge and jury when you're in the middle of the conflict, assuming someone has malicious intent and moving directly to condemnation/punishment.

When to Walk Away

Resorting to the weaknesses of your Identity Zones is self-destructive, as I mentioned previously. Unfortunately, now and then in life, we encounter individuals who are locked into a self-destructive cycle. These individuals are unreceptive to bridge building, unmoved by productive responses. No matter how well intentioned we are, we're bound to fail, because we're dealing with someone who's not open or ready to engage with us in the spirit of learning and relationship building. In the worst-case scenario, dealing with such an individual is not merely unproductive, but also potentially dangerous.

How do you recognize the signs that there are no safe crossing zones in a relationship? Sometimes we make repeated efforts, it feels like we're making no progress, and, then, suddenly, just as we're about to give up—voilà! A crossing zone opens before us, and a relationship that seemed doomed gets another chance. On the other hand, sometimes we make repeated efforts, it feels like we're making no progress, and we get a clear signal that we're correct: it's time to walk away.

I can't give you a crystal ball so that you can predict which way a certain relationship is going to go. It would be a shame to give up too quickly simply because you are uncomfortable, or because the issues are tough. But watch out when you encounter people who:

- Are verbally or physically abusive.
- Express hatred for certain groups based on affiliations or values.
- Are constantly in "attack" mode.
- Blame everyone but themselves.
- Habitually lie or distort the truth.
- Give the same speech or file the same complaint over and over again.

These are just some of the signs that the relationship is truly a mine-field. You may need to reassess your goal for the relationship and decide to focus on protecting yourself from risk. You may need to divest, keeping the relationship as transactional as possible. If you're in a position where you feel threatened and can't walk away (because you're dealing with a coworker, a boss, a family member who has situational or hierarchal power), don't hesitate: get help and get it fast, before you or somebody else gets hurt.

When difficult relationships become dangerous, when the stakes get too high for us to handle by ourselves, we are smart to reach out for intervention from other family members, from counselors or mediators, from attorneys or officers of the law, from human resource managers and other authorities.

Part 5

KNOWING YOUR PURPOSE

A human being is part of a whole, called by us the Universe, a part limited in time and space. He experiences himself, his thoughts and feelings, as something separated from the rest—a kind of optical delusion of his consciousness. This delusion is a kind of prison for us, restricting us to our personal desires and to affection for a few persons nearest us. Our task must be to free ourselves from this prison by widening our circles of compassion to embrace all living creatures and the whole of nature in its beauty.

—Albert Einstein (1879–1955)

Throughout this book, we have explored five Identity Zones: temperature, circle of inclusion, commitment, strategy, and power. I built the Identity Zones framework around these core zones, believing they are the essential pieces of the identity puzzle in the twenty-first century, the keys to unlocking the potential of relationships in today's multiage.

But as I refined the Identity Zones framework, consulting with trusted friends and advisors, I came to believe that something was missing. How could I help people connect with themselves and others on the deepest of levels? I needed to speak to another level of identity. I needed to expand the breadth and depth of the discussion, to touch upon an avenue of meaningful exploration that has been central to my own life. Eventually, I concluded that the missing "something" was a sixth zone: the Purpose Zone.

If there is indeed a sixth zone, why didn't I introduce it earlier, when you were selecting your priorities and charting your zones? The reason is simple: the nature of the Purpose Zone is radically different. The other five zones lie on a true continuum, representing a spectrum of feelings and convictions: hot or cold, open or closed, passive or activist. They are not tied to right or wrong, beginning or end, just your own personal place within each zone. There is no ideal.

We need the strengths of the hot perspective to stay sensitive, aware, and tolerant. We need the strengths of the warm perspective to maintain balance and reach compromise. And we need the strengths of the cold perspective to remain clear-headed and keep our sense of humor. The same holds true for the other zones: ideally, we seek a blending of perspectives, to capitalize on the strengths of each.

But the Purpose Zone is an evolutionary continuum. It is a measurement tool, just like the other zones, but it measures an evolutionary process. This three-stage process begins with a self-focused view of your affiliations and values, moves to a society-focused view, and evolves into a deeper understanding and awakening, what I call the soul-focused view. In this chapter, I will ask you to go back to your whole portrait and begin thinking about how you fit into this new continuum. You will ask yourself:

- What is the purpose of this affiliation or value in my life?
- What does it mean to me as a human being?
- What are the lessons to be learned from this affiliation or value?

I've highlighted the evolutionary nature of the Purpose Zone on the chart below. When we move to a soul-focused view, we become aware that our true selves are multi-selves, connected intuitively and profoundly with others in our lives and around the globe. I will discuss the concept of the multi-self in more detail at the conclusion of the book.

Temperature	Hot	Warm	Cold
Circle of Inclusion	Closed	Selective	Open
Commitment	Activist	Engaged	Passive
Strategy	Transform	Reform	Conform
Power	High	Medium	Low
Purpose	Self	Society	Soul

Stage One: Self

If life is a journey, our affiliations and values are traveling with us. We have relationships with these affiliations and values, just as we have relationships with other human beings. If they are healthy relationships, now and then we must stop to ask ourselves, what do you mean to me? Why are you in my life?

The most basic answer to this question lies at the "self" end of the continuum: I must protect and defend my affiliations and values to protect and defend myself. When we focus on the "self" end of the continuum, we are driven by an innate, passionate sense of self-preservation.

We become preoccupied with our immediate survival. By narrowing our looking glass to what is immediate, day to day, and personally relevant, we interpret life events based on our own needs, fears, and desires.

When I first started to show signs of my physical disability, all I could do was protect myself from pain and maintain enough self-esteem to make it through the school day. I wasn't ready to explore what this new affiliation meant in the grand scheme of things. I didn't have the personal resources or life experience to think about others facing similar challenges. All I could do was focus on survival.

Survival has several connotations here: physical survival, emotional survival, and intellectual survival. There is no shame in the urge for self-preservation. What choice do we have? Even when we progress to other ways of thinking, self-preservation is the beating heart of our identities, the place to which we always return in times of stress and change.

I remember one young man, Otis, who was especially cruel to me at school. He followed me through the hallways and imitated how I walked; he laughed behind my back and tried to publicly humiliate me. Some of my classmates were disgusted by Otis's behavior, but others thought it was funny and joined in. I woke up early each day, planning my strategy to avoid Otis on the bus, in the hallways, in between classes, and in the cafeteria.

I confided in a guidance counselor, but after Otis was reprimanded, the teasing only got worse. I learned how to mask my disorder, altering my walk in a way that compensated for the weakness in my lower legs. I didn't care if there were people out there with my disease, and I didn't look for any support from the disabled community. My war was private, personal, and focused on survival. I wanted to be successful in spite of my limitations, to find the confidence to keep moving forward and pursuing my dreams.

There is no shame in self-preservation, no blame in viewing our affiliations and values from the "self" end of the continuum. Sometimes it's the smartest strategy, especially when we're young and vulnerable, or any time our perceived power is low.

I have an African American friend, Maya, who still recalls with deep sadness an incident from her childhood. She used to play with the little white girl who lived next door. The girl would cross the alley that separated their house, climb over the fence, and play with Maya in her backyard. Then one day, Maya crossed the alley and went to play in the little girl's yard. The two girls wanted a drink of water. Innocently, Maya walked into the house and caused a scandal. Here was a little black girl, living in the Jim Crow South, strolling through a white family's living room, interrupting a game of bridge. The card-playing ladies were shocked. Mouths dropped open. Hands fell to the table. Maya was ordered to go home. The friendship was over.

Maya had felt the first sting of racism. It cut deep. In the coming years, more overt racism (name calling, race riots, church bombings) was like salt in an open wound. She was hurt, angry, scared, and confused by the way she was treated. Needing to move forward, needing to protect herself from expressions of hate and aggression, she isolated herself from the white community, deciding that to open herself up to potentially positive relationships was too risky. She had low power across the board: personal, situational, and societal power. She didn't have access to the personal or material resources to create change. She needed time to grow, to heal, to gather her resources so she could explore whether there was a deeper meaning to her experiences.

Purpose Indicators: Self

As you move through this section of the book, remember that you may be in different places on the purpose continuum with your many affiliations and values. When you examine your high-priority values and affiliations, here are some indicators that you are at the self end of the continuum.

- **Safety and Survival.** You are focused primarily on surviving day-to-day challenges, limitations, and barriers such as intolerance, being misunderstood, or lack of power to influence your destiny.
- **Self-Esteem.** You are focused on countering negative messages, perceptions, and actions directed toward you. Or you are focused on capitalizing on the honor and privilege this affiliation or value provides you.
- **Success and Status.** You are focused on how you can minimize the liabilities of the affiliation or value and/or how to capitalize

on its benefits to be more successful (through money, acclaim, relationships, etc.) in the world.

Moving beyond Self

We must always protect and defend ourselves. We must always survive. But if protecting the self remains our sole focus throughout our lives, we can begin to feel a profound disconnection and disengagement from the world around us. Our needs, fears, and desires overwhelm and isolate us. This tends to bring out the weaknesses of the other zone continuums, to push us toward feelings and behaviors typified by cold fronts or heat waves. When an entrenched "self" view brings out the weaknesses on the cold side of the continuum, it can lead to:

- Detachment and isolation
- Lack of sensitivity
- Lack of empathy and compassion

When an entrenched "self" view brings out the weaknesses on the hot side of the continuum, it can lead to:

- Anger and rage
- Resentment
- "Scorched earth" policies toward individuals and groups

In my case, my approach to my disability in my youth was to go cold—to change my gait, hide my disability, and shut myself off from others with similar challenges. I didn't want to be lumped in with the "handicapped kids." Rather than allowing myself to empathize with them, I chose to see myself as absolutely unique, disconnected from their pain. I felt sorry for them, but pity is not the same as empathy. Over time I grew cold enough to live in denial, shutting myself off from an aspect of myself that I chose to reject.

In Maya's case, her approach to race in her youth was to go hot—to let anger and resentment take over, to blame and distrust all white people. Even when she saw evidence that some white people were not racist, she was reluctant to let down her defenses. She was justifiably angry. But over time this anger became too heavy a burden, preventing her from taking positive action and opening herself to the potential of societal change.

That's the danger of staying stuck at the "self" end of the purpose continuum. We become trapped in a self-made lens that magnifies our needs, fears, and desires. We become like the lover consumed by passion and jealousy, so focused on keeping the relationship alive that we no longer experience the joy of companionship, the power of intimacy, the strength of partnership. We lose our sense of purpose.

The self-preservation trap becomes more debilitating as we age, as the body breaks down and the mind loses its sharpness and speed. Consider the story of Daryl, a white man in his mid-fifties. As long as I've known him, Daryl aspired to be a mover and a shaker. He works in a demanding, impersonal, and—some would say—ruthless industry. People in his position are judged solely on their ability to win at all costs and make lots of money. Daryl justifies any behavior by saying it's "just business." He believes that people are motivated purely by self-interest. To play Daryl's game, you must be dispassionate about people, hide your emotions, and never display vulnerability.

Daryl has become so good at this game that his professional image has permeated every fiber of his being. He is the same driven, unemotional mover and shaker wherever he goes. He now has money, prestige, power, a wonderful family, and a beautiful home in an upscale neighborhood. Daryl is proud of his salary, his talent, and the accumulated accoutrements of an elite lifestyle. He has a network of admiring colleagues. But in the past few years, Daryl has begun to feel a little tired and empty. At this point in his life, Daryl looks back on his career and wonders what went wrong. The truth is, he did not reach all of his goals. His bank account is not as large as it could be—not in comparison to those who have more zeros. Daryl has had to manage tremendous stress during very difficult economic times. The weight of his goals has begun pressing down on him, leaving him with little breathing room.

A prolonged focus on the self often leads to loneliness, feelings of isolation and stress, and a pervasive fear of infirmity and death. Stress and loneliness have been biologically linked to an erosion of our immune systems, and they may significantly fuel certain chronic, degenerative diseases. Over time, a relentless drive toward self-preservation significantly lessens our vitality. A growing body of medical literature supports this point.

For our emotional and mental well-being, then, we do well to consider our relationship to our affiliations and values from a broader perspective. This allows for a natural progression toward the social- and soul-focused end of the purpose continuum.

Stage Two: Society

Human beings are social creatures. When we feel less threatened, sociability balances our instinct for self-preservation. We focus on the societal implications of our affiliations and values. We crave connection and companionship. We identity with groups of people according to our race, our religion, our gender, our nationality, our commitment to values such as nature, leisure, humor, or generosity. We see these social groups as an extension of ourselves and the preservation of the group as an extension of self-preservation. In the middle of the Purpose Zone, we take a longer view, sacrificing short-term coping strategies, advantages or privileges because we feel strong enough to go the distance.

Here's where the evolutionary aspect of the Purpose Zone comes in. Why is it preferable to move from a self-focus to a social focus? A social focus connects us to the world outside ourselves. It puts our needs, desires, and fears into perspective. Medicine validates this point as well: support groups and social affiliations enhance our health and vitality.

I mentioned that my friend Maya's anger about racial intolerance became a heavy burden for her. Later in life, she began to lift this burden by shifting the focus of her attention from herself to others in her situation. As her perception of her personal and societal power increased, she felt empowered to begin fighting discrimination within society. She went to work for the EEOC (Equal Employment Opportunity Commission) and joined groups that encouraged black pride and social/political change. She began demanding equality, not just for herself, but for all African Americans.

This required that she work side by side with white colleagues, if not in trust and companionship, then at least with civility and tolerance. She had to abandon her "scorched earth" policy in order to implement societal change. Her anger didn't go away, but she found an outlet that helped make her pain and anger useful.

Personally, I have found the move from self to society with respect to my disability a tremendous relief. I've only just begun to acknowledge the reality of my connection to a larger group of disabled people. With this acknowledgment, I feel less haunted by the fears that crowded my mind the moment the disease reawakened. (How will I cope? How will my family cope? What about my career?) I used to notice handicapped parking spaces and feel afraid, wondering if and when I would ever need one. Not long ago, I saw a car parked illegally in a handicapped space. For the first time, I felt a tinge of anger—a flare based in solidarity and empathy, imagining how frustrating it must be to deal with other people's lack of awareness. Since that triggering event, I'm beginning to think more about disability laws, access, insurance, and other issues that impact people with disabilities. As I learn to "own" my affiliation on disability, I can imagine joining a support group to help track such issues and broaden my awareness.

I don't mean to suggest that I have left the "self" area on the continuum behind. Believe me, I'm still focused on self-preservation, still concerned and sometimes fearful of the future. Dr. Don Beck, author of *Spiral Dynamics,* is a friend and colleague. He says,

> When a new worldview emerges, the previously awakened stages do not disappear. Rather, they remain subsumed in their total flow, and not only add texture to the more complex ways of living, but remain "on call" in case the problems that first awakened them to service reappear.

In times of stress, or when anticipating change, I still tend to personalize disability issues. (Can I travel in comfort? Will I need leg braces? How can I protect myself from a potentially catastrophic fall? Will my family need to move when I can no longer negotiate the stairs in my house?) But I find that my fears subside when I think of myself as part of a group, when I can channel my fears into empathy, understanding, and positive energy for change.

Purpose Indicators: Society

- **Strength and Solidarity.** When you think of this affiliation or value, you think about a community of people. You think of shared traditions, customs, experiences, and support for one another. You are invested in protecting, defending, improving, or contributing to the welfare and well-being of the entire group. You see their triumphs and defeats as connected to your life experience.
- **Social Esteem.** When you think about your affiliation and value, you're concerned about your group's social status—its place in the pecking order, its ranking in relation to other groups. You're focused on changing or reinforcing how your group is perceived and portrayed, the common assumptions and mis-perceptions.
- **Systems.** You are focused on ways to either reinforce or improve your groups' political, economic, and institutional power. You feel more comfortable when people who share your affiliation/value are major stakeholders in societal institutions.

Stage Three: Soul

How can we become fully alive? According to the philosopher and psychologist Carl Jung (1875–1961), we can try to live through the passion of our soul.

Carl Jung's theories of personality have influenced countless contemporary thinkers and writers, including Katharine Briggs and her daughter, Isabel Briggs Myers, creators of the now famous Myers-Briggs Type Indicator. Many people have come to associate Jung primarily with the distinction between introverts and extroverts, and ways each of us prefer to deal with our inner and outer worlds (sensing vs. intuiting, thinking vs. feeling, and so forth).

Jung's work encompasses many aspects of human experience, however, and he spent a great deal of his life exploring questions of self, soul, and consciousness. He believed it was possible to live life "in tune" with your own soul, a process he called individuation. When you are most authentic, most connected to your true self, soul tendencies become expressed in daily activities. Your external behavior mirrors your internal self. You feel more fully alive, because you define self according to innate, powerful drives.

At the soul end of the Purpose continuum, we begin to see our affiliations and values as vehicles that offer valuable lessons. We recognize a greater purpose to life and become part of a divine or universal order; in other words, we are meant to be the way we are. There are no accidents. Our affiliations and values are present for a reason. We retain the drive for self-preservation and socialization, but our commitment shifts toward finding connections, letting go of external distinctions, seeking an understanding of our place in a larger context—community, world, the universe itself. As I approach this place on the continuum, my disability will take on new meaning when I begin to grapple with such questions as:

- Why do I have this disease?
- What is its purpose in my life?
- What lessons will I learn from it?
- What lessons have I already learned from it?
- How does this disease connect me to the whole of humanity?

Seeking our purpose is not easy. But at the Soul end of the continuum, we feel powerful enough, and evolved enough, to try anyway. We use private reflection and self-discovery to explore. We use our relationship with others, with our time and place, to gain understanding. We use all the tools we have, including faith and love, to appreciate the process. Thomas Moore, author of *Care of the Soul*, explains:

> One's soulful journey is not about curing the soul, but about perpetual care. We are not solving the puzzle of life, but rather appreciating the paradoxical mysteries that go into its grandeur.

This end of the continuum is about translating our life experiences, whatever they may be—pain, sorrow, rejection, oppression, privilege—into wisdom.

If we use soulful metaphors and symbols to put life in perspective, we can tap into a global, timeless source of energy. We gain an invisible family of ancestors, those who have come before us and those who will come after, all struggling with the same life issues. Our daily experience is not unique but universal. The soul end of the continuum is about aligning your life with your values—reverence, compassion, forgiveness, generosity, service, sacrifice, and, ultimately, love.

Here is how Maya describes the "soul lessons" she gained through race, lessons whose seeds were sewn was she was a little girl in South Carolina, devastated by a single intolerant act.

- Don't reflect the thing you dislike in others. I had become a reflection of the very thing that I disliked in Sara's parents. They showed displeasure and discomfort when I was around and created distance between Sara and I. Because of this experience and others like it, I was reluctant to establish relationships with white people and often distanced myself from them. Sure, I went to school and managed a certain level of courtesy and tolerance, but my trust had been betrayed. I did not like being vulnerable, so I resisted any efforts on their part to build meaningful friendships. I had swallowed the discomfort and distance of Sara's parents, and now I spat it back out at the world. This was a very difficult lesson to accept.
- Don't wait for others to earn your trust; assume they are doing the best they can, and honor them by giving them unconditional respect. This was another difficult lesson. I knew what distrust felt like, but I had no idea how hard it would be for white people to earn my trust. Neither did they. Try as they might, they could never break through my barrier. I was willing to offer plenty of conditional respect ("I will tolerate you as long as you act like I think you should act"), but I offered no unconditional respect. And that's exactly what I wanted from others. I learned to honor all people because they are fellow human beings, struggling to find their way. Conditional respect is still important, because it

demands accountability. But without unconditional respect there is no human dignity.

- Stop stereotyping and see people as the individuals they are. I wasted valuable time and abandoned some relationships that may have been very important in my soul's development because I thought all white people were the same. But we are just souls packaged in our physical bodies. This package does not always dictate our values, fears, challenges, gifts, or needs.

- Find the positive traits behind negative behaviors, then embrace them. The negative that you see in others is likely to be a positive that has been overemphasized or disproportionately twisted. Sara's parents acted superior and treated Maya as if she were not good enough to associate with their daughter. This superiority is an excessive expression of self-confidence and self-assurance. While I did not want to adopt a superior attitude, I needed to develop self-confidence and self-assurance. I knew that these traits lay somewhere between superiority and inferiority, and I had to extract them from the continuum.

- Understand and appreciate your life's purpose; use it to structure your relationships. Until I understood my personal purpose—to expand the mind and elevate the spirit—I'd find myself slipping into small-minded thinking and engaging in behaviors that injured my spirit. I was angry and resentful of white people until I recognized that each resentful, bitter, and angry thought or action violated my life's purpose and dishonored my soul. Understanding my purpose led me to question, and ultimately discard, these undermining behaviors.

We should see human beings as they truly are: each on her own journey, struggling with deep universal issues. I don't care more about society or group issues than I do my own, but I bring all these degrees of consciousness with me to the soul perspective. From the soul perspective we have achieved true solidarity, everyone becomes our brother and sister and part of our family, whether they are in Bangladesh or the Upper East Side of New York, whether they are in a housing project in Chicago or a village in Iraq. We see everyone as a part of the universal soul. "Soul" demands taking responsibility for our actions because an invisible web connects us all. Large problems, such as oppression and intolerance, can shift because two people choose to act. Each word, act, and thought ripples out through our relationships, our community, and our world.

Carl Jung pointed out that children search for differentiation, seeking to find out the difference between one thing and another, always asking, what's this, what's that? The goal of adult development is different. We search to integrate experiences, to transcend opposites. Adults are in a quest to find out how things and people contribute to the whole. We want to make sense of our experiences, find the meaning in our lives, and discover the purpose of our existence. As children, we unravel the world. As adults, we try to knit it back together.

Purpose Indicators: Soul

- **Symbolic Interpretations.** You may focus on translating your literal experiences into symbolic images such as metaphors, archetypes, and imagery to find the universal in the everyday.
- **Spiritual Journey.** You may strive to accept the blessings, limitations, and experiences that relate to your affiliation/value as gifts designed to help you evolve into your higher self. You may start to believe that the material worldly aspects of your existence are only one dimension of your reality, and stop focusing on the "things" that your affiliation/value does or doesn't help you obtain.
- **Shared Humanity.** You may believe that your affiliation/value connects you to a human family. Life, death, sorrow, joy, triumphs, and defeats are all a part of the human experience regardless of our cultural differences. We are connected to each other and we have a profound responsibility to each other to act with integrity, love, and justice.

Exercise: Soul

Use one of your key affiliations or values to reflect on the soul lessons—if any—that you have learned. Write your answers down in a journal.

Purpose is a unique zone; it indicates the scope of our focus on an affiliation—whether it is self-based, society-based, or an entirely soulful pursuit. In this excerpt from our national survey, notice how married, divorced, and single people described their purpose when it comes to parental status.

ZONE: PURPOSE
AFFILIATION: PARENTAL STATUS

	Married	Divorced, Separated, Widowed	Single
Soul	37.5%	33.4%	21.4%
Society	30.4%	23.2%	25.5%
Self	25.0%	30.1%	29.3%

Source: Zogby Survey
03/15/04–03/22/04
Margin of Error: +/–3.1%

20

The Age of
the Multi-self

As promised, I've returned to the subject of the multi-self. Now that you're aware of the Purpose zone, now that we've discussed the soul perspective, we have the proper context for the multi-self. I believe contemporary society (by which I mean "global society" is moving along an evolutionary continuum with respect to identity. I don't claim to know or understand all the points along this particular continuum.

But I do believe, as I said at this book's beginning, that we are in the process of moving from the uni-self age to the multi-self age. Old ways of understanding and interacting—with friends, with family, and with ourselves—are proving less successful in this society. One era is ending, another beginning. Certainly, we can expect many swings of the pendulum, many cycles of growth followed by cycles of fear and reversion, much as we can expect periods of "self" focus in our evolution toward the soul perspective. But with the proliferation of acceptable affiliations and values, we are being asked to make a choice: adapt and move forward, or retrench and be left behind. If you choose, as I do, to adapt to the age of the multi-self, I would like to put forward five main principles we can be guided by. Of course, you are invited to add your own principles to this list, building your own vision of a more soulful life.

- **Search for the Whole Human Being.** See all aspects of a person: physical and visible differences, values and core beliefs, ties to cultural traditions, affiliations with different groups, acceptance of (and deviance from) group norms. Try to understand a person's worldview and perspective, including his deeper spiritual beliefs about the purpose of life. Believe that all these factors contribute to the authenticity of human relationships.
- **Search for the Inner Prize.** Understand the essence of the other. Peel back the different aspects of identity. Learn how individuals prioritize their values and affiliations—and how they manage interrelationships and conflicts among various aspects of their identity—to deepen the connection.
- **Search for Commonality.** Don't focus exclusively on difference. Seek out and cultivate commonalities in order to motivate, bond, and build community. Life is filled with shared experiences at the very deepest levels. Our personal connection with others is often based on a shared affiliation or value. Our shared humanity is the common thread that unites us all.
- **Search for Compassion.** Help others, change your behavior, make sacrifices, and forgive. Everyone has challenges to overcome. Cultivate a sense of reverence and awe about your connection to your family, neighborhood, workplace, community, and world.
- **Search for Growth.** The "other" often sheds light on our blind spots, so we may operate with greater awareness. Approach each person as a mirror that may reflect an undiscovered or unrealized aspect of your own identity. Use your affiliations and values as vehicles for learning. Never stop exploring, investigating, and learning about others or yourself.

About the Author

For more than 20 years, Mark A. Williams has been improving human interactions and organizational effectiveness for such clients as AT&T, UNISYS, Avon, American Express, Marriott International, Microsoft, Sara Lee, Central Intelligence Agency, Agency for International Development, and Harvard Medical School. He is the founding partner of MarkusWorks, a research and consulting firm focused on human identity issues, and a partner with John Zogby in the Zogby-Williams Institute for the Study of Human Identity. Mark Williams has been quoted widely in such publications as *Fast Company, Black Enterprise, San Francisco Chronicle, Chicago Tribune,* and *Boston Globe,* and has been interviewed on Bloomberg News, CBS Early Show, CNN Financial News Network, and others. He is Chairman of the One Song, Many Voices Foundation, and founded The Diversity Channel, an eLearning, training, and education service. In 1998 he was honored with the Global Tolerance Award from the Friends of the United Nations. Mark Williams is the author of *The 10 Lenses: Your Guide to Living & Working in a Multicultural World* (Capital, 2001).

Index